Beavers

Water, Wildlife and History

Beavers

Water, Wildlife and History

Text and Photographs
by

Earl L. Hilfiker

Windswept Press
Interlaken, New York
1991

Library of Congress Cataloging-in-Publication Data

Hilfiker, Earl L., 1902–
   Beavers : water, wildlife, and history / by Earl L. Hilfiker.
   198 p.   cm.
   Includes bibliographical references.
   1. Beavers.   2. Beavers—Ecology.   3. Fur   trade—North
America—History.   I. Title.
QL737.R632H54 1991   599.32'32—dc20   90-12698

ISBN: 1-55787-067-5
ISBN: 1-55787-068-3 (paperback)
Manufactured in the United States

A *quality* publication of
Heart of the Lakes Publishing
Interlaken, New York 14847

Dedication

This book is dedicated to my wife, Beulah A. Hilfiker. Over the years she has been my companion on expeditions, many off the beaten path where we observed and photographed wildlife. And to my parents, Lewis W. Hilfiker and Grace M. Hilfiker who gave me the encouragement to pursue my interest in wildlife and the opportunity to get an education that circumstances had denied them.

Contents

Foreword

My interest in beavers and their works began many years ago, when I saw my first beaver pond in the Adirondack Mountains just as beavers were beginning to become re-established in parts of their former range. There are those who believe that the beaver is a shy, furtive creature that avoids man, shuns anything that bears human odor, and does its work only at night under the cover of darkness. Fortunately for those interested in observing and photographing beavers, there are in fact times and places where beaver behavior is quite different. During approximately four and a half decades of travel as a wildlife photographer, it has been my good fortune to film the beaver and his works in many places across North America.

My close association with the beaver began in 1940. At that time, the organization then known as The Rochester Museum of Arts and Sciences was housed in an old building in Edgerton Park, but plans were being made to build a new structure on the Edward Bausch property on East Avenue. Among the new exhibits was to be a large diorama of a beaver pond at the south end of the hall on the main floor. In the summer of that year at the New York State Fair in Syracuse, the New York State Department of Conservation had on display a living family of beavers, which they had agreed to give to the museum for its diorama upon the conclusion of the fair.

At the appointed time, I drove the museum's station wagon to Syracuse to pick them up. Originally, they had been a family of five, but one adult had died, leaving one adult and three kits. Before I went, I built a fence around the small fish pond in my parents' back yard in the Town of Parma. Upon my return from Syracuse, the beavers settled into their new home.

Every afternoon I drove out to feed them. Fortunately, a neighbor had a stand of aspens on her property a quarter of a mile away so with her permission, I cut and dragged to the pond enough of the aspens to feed the beavers. This went on for several weeks, and I learned that a beaver family can consume a large quantity of food.

They were in their summer coats, and it would be several months before they would become prime. Moreover, they had become pampered pets, and the thought of killing them was becoming increasingly repugnant. Suddenly, I was struck with what at the time appeared to be a brilliant solution to the problem. We had four beavers that were accustomed to human presence. Would it not be an excellent idea to release them in a place where people could come and watch beavers at work? To me, Mendon Ponds County Park seemed to be ideal.

Arthur C. Parker was the director of the museum at the time, and so I called at his office and presented my idea. He was sympathetic, and his response was "I do not wish to see them butchered either. See what you can do." As a result, there was a conference with the County Director of Parks, Robert Cochrane. He agreed that the idea had possibilities, but he added this restriction: "If they cause a problem, we have a gentlemen's agreement that you will immediately remove them." Although I was not sure how it could be done, we shook hands, and I agreed to the conditions.

The next day they were released in a small body of water known as Deep Pond, which created an ideal situation for park visitors to observe them. This was probably the first time in over two hundred years that there were beavers swimming in that pond.

The next morning I had a call from Julius White, who at the time was in charge of a quail restoration project and the various other wildlife projects in the park. He said, "Earl, we have a problem." The problem was that the first night the beavers cut down an eight-inch poplar that was growing beside the road. His comment was, "See what your damn butchers did." I cut up the tree and threw it in the pond.

A few days later I received another call. Two of the young ones had been trying to get through an outlet tile, and one of the park workmen had blocked the end with stones and drowned them.

The two remaining beavers built a house close to the road and started cutting down the poplar trees that grew near it. I made another trip to the park to destroy the evidence and once again cut up the trees and threw them in the pond. It so happened that there was a stand of poison sumac growing there. I failed to recognize it, however, and the cost of destroying the evidence this time was three days in bed with sumac poisoning—not a pleasant experience.

The next spring the beavers decided to move downstream to a point between Hundred Acre Pond and Mud Pond where a seldom-used service road crossed a low-lying area. WPA workers had dug a series of duck ponds there, and the results of their efforts were a couple of shallow holes a couple of feet deep, neither larger than a football field. Ducks never used them for the best of reasons: there was never water in them. The beavers, however, built a dam immediately above the small bridge across the road and created a pond of several acres in extent which ducks and other waterfowl did use, as did fish, frogs, and turtles.

At a later date, the beavers moved downstream again and occupied a seldom-visited part of the park, Mud Pond. In the meantime, I moved out of the area, and it was six years before I returned. Whether or not beavers still live there, I do not know.

My next opportunity to photograph and film the members of a beaver family and their activities came several years later, where in the Canadian National Park a short distance from Banff, Alberta, Canada, a beaver pond constituted one of the chief tourist attractions. Every morning, the park rangers cut aspen and cottonwood saplings and threw them into the pond, and every afternoon, when the light was still good for picture-taking, the beaver family came out to feed upon and work up the material that the rangers had provided. The pond was close to what was then the main road, and the beavers went about their work, paying no attention to the large numbers of spectators who were watching and the photographers who were recording them at work.

A number of years later and many miles distant, I had another extraordinary opportunity to observe and photograph a family of beavers at work. This family lived in France Brook, a small stream in Allegany State Park in the southwest corner of New York State, and I spent considerable amounts of time with them over a period of five years. Every afternoon they came out from their lodge, went to work, and were not in the least disturbed by the presence of the people who were watching them. Although this was the only beaver family living along France Brook, evidence of their presence could be seen for about a quarter of a mile downstream and approximately half a mile upstream. Within that area they maintained twelve dams of various sizes, dug out canals, rebuilt an abandoned house upstream, lived in it one winter, and then moved back into the original house downstream.

At one point, trappers killed several members of the beaver family, but enough survived to carry on the work. In March of the fifth year, however, trappers were permitted to take the entire family. The summer after the beavers were killed, France Brook, which always had water in it when the beavers were living there, went dry for several weeks. The following year, another pair of beavers moved in at the headwaters of the brook and reoccupied a pond that had been abandoned five years before. In stark contrast to the family before them, this family was suspicious of man and resented human presence. They expressed this resentment by slapping the water with their tails, and on a number of occasions I recorded this action on film.

Life has a way of coming full-circle. In 1826, my great great-grandfather, Joseph Vinton, and a group of his relatives moved their families from Connecticut to western New York State. They carried their possessions in ox carts and followed a route marked by ax blazes on the trunks of trees. They settled around Irondequoit Bay in the area that now makes up the Towns of Irondequoit, Webster, and Penfield. When they arrived, they found themselves in a magnificent hardwood forest. Within less than two decades, however, except for small woodlots, most of the trees were gone, and the larger forms of wildlife had disappeared. The beaver had disappeared or become very rare many years before they even left Connecticut.

Some eighty years later, when I was five years old, my family moved out of Rochester to a small community about eight miles to the west known as Parma Corners. My father had bought a grist mill on Northrup Creek that had been built by a member of the Sperry Family who came from Connecticut with Joseph Vinton. He converted the building into an apple evaporator. We lived in a house diagonally across the road from the mill, and I spent many hours in, on, and around the pond and on expeditions up and down the creek. In so doing, by osmosis, I developed an abiding interest in the outdoors and with it, I hope, some knowledge of the ways of nature.

About the only forms of wildlife I ever saw on those expeditions were an occasional Woodchuck, Eastern Cottontail Rabbit, Muskrat, Red Squirrel, or Ringneck Pheasant. Because of their nocturnal habits, they were seldom seen, but there were occasions when there was pungent and irrefutable evidence that skunks were also a part of our resident wildlife population.

Had anyone told us that we would see the day when the suburbs of Rochester would have a deer herd out of control and beavers living within the city limits, we would never have believed it. Nevertheless, that has come to pass. In my lifetime, I have seen the return of the Whitetailed Deer, Black Bear, Beaver, Wild Turkey, and other forms of wildlife that had disappeared from western New York. And since work was started on this book, beavers have moved back into Northrup Creek, built dams, and set up housekeeping within a few hundred yards below the location of the former mill pond and the house where I lived for several years when we first moved to Parma.

1

The North American Beaver

Of all the creatures of creation, only two have the special ability to make major changes in their environment and alter it to suit their special needs. One is man, the other, the beaver. It would be most difficult to find a creature less human in appearance, yet so like man in many of his traits and accomplishments. He mates for life. He is a faithful husband and a devoted parent. Beaver family life is of a very high order. The young stay with the family until after the second winter.

The beaver is a most provident creature. In times of plenty an ample food supply is stored up against the family's time of need. He is a skilled lumberjack, an expert logger, and a very clever engineer. He builds dams, maintains ponds, clears roadways, excavates tunnels, digs canals, and conducts extensive lumbering and logging operations.

The house the beaver builds is the best constructed that is built by any creature except man. When put in the middle of the pond, it becomes a moated castle where the family is safe from surprise attack at any season of the year, and it gives special protection in winter when it is frozen hard as concrete and proof against the teeth and claws of the strongest and most determined enemy.

The beaver's appearance is definitely not impressive. It is the things he does rather than his appearance that make him one of the most widely recognized forms of North American wildlife and the one whose picture so frequently appears on the faces of greeting cards. Yet, the average individual knows very little about the beaver and his accomplishments. If asked to describe the beaver, his answer might be, "The beaver is a cute little animal that builds dams and works all the time."

Because he must carry around a very large digestive system and its contents, the beaver is squat, rotund and generally clumsy in his movements. His normal gait is a waddling walk. If hard pressed, his fastest speed is an awkward quadruped gallop. He cannot travel fast on land, and a person in reasonably good physical condition can easily run him down.

France Brook Pond, early summer.

There are times, however, when the beaver's actions make one forget his dumpy appearance and awkward movements. In nature, the price of survival is ceaseless vigilance. If there is the slightest hint of anything unusual, the beaver stands erect, draws himself up to his full height, turns his head, and sniffs the air to detect the faintest odor. He watches for any suspicious movement and pricks up his ears to detect the direction of a sound that might betray the approach of an enemy. If fully satisfied, he resumes whatever he has been doing. If not, he seeks safety in the water. During those moments when he assumes that position, the beaver becomes a creature of majesty and beauty.

Another occasion is when one is fortunate enough to observe him at work. He then becomes the epitome of efficiency. He wastes no movement, and he accomplishes his tasks with a minimum of effort. A third time is when the beaver is in the water. When swimming on the surface or when submerged, he glides through the water with effortless ease, and his movements there are in sharp contrast with his awkward progress on the land.

Size

The beaver is the largest rodent native to North America, and it is the second largest rodent in the world. Only the capybara of South

12

America grows to a larger size. The body grows to an approximate length of forty inches from the tip of the nose to the end of the tail. Excluding the tail stalk, the broad end or blade of the tail is approximately twelve inches long. The weight of an adult is from thirty-five to forty pounds. A fifty animal is considered very large. However, there are records of very rare individuals weighing over one hundred pounds.

Vernon Bailey (3) made some interesting comments concerning beaver ages and weights. He recorded a three-year-old female beaver caught near Ashland, Wisconsin as weighing fifty pounds and measuring forty-two and one-half inches in length. In addition, he noted the following generalizations of age and weight.

Age	Weight in Pounds
Birth	1
3 weeks	1.5–2
6 weeks	4
1 year	25–30
3 years	50
Old animals	60–70

He also noted records of old and fat beavers weighing one hundred pounds and one weighing one hundred ten pounds.

Range and Classification

Most people think of the beaver as strictly American. Salverson stated, "In earlier times the beaver inhabited a large area in both the Old and the New World. In Europe, they appeared in all countries except Ireland. In Asia, they reached the Euphrates River." In 1868, Morgan (14) wrote,

> The habitat of the European beaver was as wide as that of the American. He was found in the British Isles, in all parts of the European Continent, in Siberia and southward in Asia Minor to the Euphrates. He is now extinct in Europe except on some of the larger rivers of the continent and in some parts of Russia. In Scotland and Wales he was found as late as the twelfth century. He is still found in Siberia.

The beavers of Eurasia and North America were originally classified as members of the same species, *Castor fiber*, of the family Castoridae by Linnaeus, who founded the genus in 1735. Subsequently, they were assigned to separate species: the American Beaver was known as *Castor canadensis*, and the Eurasian as *Castor fiber*. Now, however, once again only a single species is considered valid, *Castor fiber*, but several subspecies are recognized from each continent. Those from Eurasia include the Scandinavian Beaver *(Castor fiber fiber)*; the Elbe Beaver *(C.*

13

f. albicus); the Rhone Beaver *(C. f. galliae);* the Polish or Byelorussian Beaver *(C. f. vistulanus);* the Ural Beaver *(C. f. pohlei);* the Mongolian Beaver *(C. f. birulai).* In North America, the Canadian Beaver *(C. f. canadensis);* the Michigan Beaver *(C. f. michiganensis);* the Newfoundland Beaver *(C. f. caecator);* the Rio Grande Beaver *(C. f. frondator);* and the Golden-bellied Beaver *(C. f. subauratus),* among others, are recognized (9).

Anatomically Eurasian and North American beavers may be identical, but their behaviors are dramatically different. The beavers of Europe and Asia never developed the engineering skills of the beavers of North America. There are places in the taiga of Asiatic Russia where one may see extensive beaver works, but these have been accomplished by beavers whose ancestors were imported from North America.

The American beaver had a special advantage over its Old World counterpart in that it had many centuries to develop engineering skills before the first humans found their way across the Bering Peninsula from Asia. Wherever water stood or flowed and poplars and willows grew, the beaver was completely at home. There was even a race that adapted to life in the prairies and were known as grass beavers. Undoubtedly there were sparse growths of willow shrubs growing along the water courses, but in the absence of trees, these animals built their dams and lodges out of sod, mud, and stones.

Of all the forms of wildlife native to North America, only cougars had a range larger than that occupied by beavers. This covered an area of approximately 7.5 million square miles. It included most of present-day Alaska, Canada, the lower forty-eight states of the United States, and for a considerable distance it extended down into the mountains of present-day Mexico. Within that range lived many millions of beavers. To estimate their average population density per square mile and their total number would be a matter of pure conjecture. It is true that there were large expanses of prime beaver country that supported a number of families per square mile. It is equally true that the extreme northern part of the continent is covered with treeless tundra where only thin layers of vegetation cover the permafrost beneath. One must also consider the extensive deserts of the southwestern United States and northern Mexico. Then too, in the Rocky Mountains only the valleys and lower elevations could have supported beavers, but today in some of those places can be seen the most extensive and interesting works of beavers that can be found anywhere in the world.

Population Estimates

One can only estimate the number of beavers per square mile and the total number of the beaver population. However, because of the

Beaver ponds near the headwaters of the Colorado River, Rocky Mountain National Park, Colorado. This series of beaver ponds provides excellent fishing for Eastern Book Trout. For miles downstream, this upper stream valley is terraced with beaver ponds.

size of the former range, one might safely conclude that before the arrival of the Europeans, the beaver population was larger than that of the buffalo for which there are estimates of from sixty to eighty million.

There is a wide range of opinions among those who have studied the beaver and written about him. They have estimated the former population density per square mile and calculated the total beaver population of North America accordingly. Grzimek (9) says the United States once had sixty million beavers. Hodgdon and Hunt (11) quoted Ernest Thompson Seaton's estimate which ranges from sixty per square mile to five or six per square mile. "With a beaver colony every one to three miles and six to nine beavers per colony, Maine's primitive numbers of beavers would have been 36,000 to 162,000."

Vernon Bailey's (3) comments on former beaver numbers are also interesting. "The area occupied was approximately six million square miles, and probably two hundred beaver per square mile would be a conservative estimate." Bailey's estimates would put the prehistoric beaver population at 1,200,000,000 individuals.

15

On the basis of two families of six or eight per square mile across Canada and the United States, including Alaska, we would arrive at an estimate of a prehistoric beaver population of from 90,000,000 to 120,000,000.

Beavers seldom travel far from their home territory; therefore, within the enormous range that they originally occupied, a number of strains or races, now identified as subspecies, evolved. Those in the southern part of the range were generally smaller in size and had poorer quality fur. To the north, individuals were progressively larger, darker in color, and had heavier, denser fur.

Many races of beavers were exterminated at an early date. The most highly prized skins were those of the rare black beavers, and they accordingly brought the highest prices in the fur auctions of London. The greatest numbers of black beavers came from the vicinity of Churchill in Manitoba, Canada, on the west side of Hudson Bay. There are also mentions of spotted beavers, but their skins were regarded as of inferior quality.

Next to the rare black beavers, the skins that brought the highest average prices were those of the Lake Superior or Michigan Beaver from the Upper Peninsula of Michigan and Wisconsin. Both the Michigan and the Canadian Beavers have fur of higher quality than do the Missouri Beavers, which are represented by those now living in Yellowstone National Park and along the Missouri River. The beavers that live in North America today are chiefly descendents of these three subspecies.

Prehistoric Beavers

Ancestors of the present-day beaver appeared many thousands of years ago during the Pleistocene Era. Morgan (14) reported, "Beaver-gnawed wood was found in the same cavity with, and five feet above he skeleton of the mastodon discovered in 1867, at Cohoes, near Albany, New York." The remains of gigantic fossil beavers have been found in Ohio (hence the name, *Castoroides ohioensis)* and in Wayne County, New York. From these, scientists estimate that this ancestor must have been bear-sized, or from five to six times larger than the beavers we know today. Another smaller ancestral form, yet larger than present-day beavers, has been named *Castor californiensis,* reflecting the fact that its remains were found in California.

During the period that followed the retreat of the glaciers, the Beaver shared its range with creatures like the Cave Bear, the Dire Wolf, Giant Bison, the Giant Sloth, and the Wooly Mammoth. Unlike these forms, which are now extinct, the Beaver was highly successful in adapting to the changing conditions of the environment.

es are very highly developed.

tely small, the optic nerve a
smallest in the skull. As his
on it except with reference
hearing is very acute. The
ch in length, terminates in a
globular form, and large
considerably larger than in
the measure of this sense.

ability to see well under water.
t a handicap to an animal that
nge. Even the keenest vision on
There, even standing erect, it is
egetation. Little is known about
on must certainly be adequate
done during the hours of

hearing is unusually acute. The
de and out, and equipped with
e submerges and reopen when
he use a point of high ground as
would stand erect, sniff the air,
ghtest movement or the faintest
nd, in addition to his ability to
sense the approach of danger from the special senses of hearing and
smell, the beaver makes use of the very sensitive nerves in its hind feet
that can detect the slightest vibrations of the earth that might signal the
approach of an enemy.

The beaver's sense of smell is also well developed. It can sniff out
the location of a body of water or a stand of trees at a considerable
distance. It may come out of its pond, sit up, sniff the air, and make a
direct route to a stand of poplars two hundred yards distant. Again,
guided by smell, it retraces that first route followed until it becomes a
well-worn trail.

The nose is equipped with a pair of flap valves which close
automatically when the beaver dives or swims and reopen when it
resurfaces. These valves keep out the water, but in no way do they
interfere with the animal's ability to smell under water. Its ability to see,
hear, smell, and taste when submerged, combined with its ability to
detect the slightest vibration, guide the beaver's movements under

water when light is limited and even absent altogether. These senses enable the animal to avoid danger to the point where even under water, a trap-wise animal can detect the scent on objects that have been handled by humans.

These highly developed special senses are extremely helpful to beavers living in the northernmost part of their range, which extends well beyond the limit of the timberline into the tundra of the Arctic. There, for half the year, the ponds are covered with ice up to two feet thick, and the ice in turn is covered with snow. Little if any light can penetrate this cover, and for six months of the year, all activities must be carried on under conditions of partial to complete darkness.

Fur

Another of Nature's special gifts to the beaver is its marvelous fur coat, which serves its owner in a number of ways. As an overcoat it keeps its owner warm in the coldest weather. As a raincoat it keeps the beaver dry even when it is under water. It serves as a life jacket to keep him afloat, and it affords considerable protection against the teeth and claws of enemies. That coat is in two layers. On the outside are the ends of the long, coarse guard hairs. Under them, next to the skin, is a dense layer of underfur. Many fur-bearers, such as the mink, have fur that becomes prime in November, but this is not so for the beaver or the muskrat. Their fur does not become prime until March, the time when water temperatures are the lowest.

That marvelous fur coat requires constant care. If neglected, it will mat down and become waterlogged, in which event the owner might die of exposure. The beaver uses the claws of its front feet to clean and comb its coat, and on the second toe of the hind foot is a special claw that serves as another kind of comb. Beavers spend long periods of time in caring for their fur. After it is cleaned, combed out, and rubbed dry, it is waterproofed with droplets of oil taken from the special oil glands located at the base of the tail.

Legs and Feet

As mentioned at the outset, on land, the beaver is slow and clumsy, and its normal gait is a waddling walk. When forced to travel faster, this may be increased to an awkward trot. If hard pressed, the beaver breaks into a lumbering quadruped gallop. At best, his gait is slow. Normally he travels on all four feet, but he can and frequently does walk upright, especially when carrying mud, stones, or other materials in his arms.

The hind legs of the beaver are very powerful and are much larger and more heavily muscled than the front legs. The feet are unusually

A closeup view of the hind foot of an adult beaver. The split claw on the second toe can be clearly seen.

large, have five toes, and are fully webbed. They can easily be injured by walking over sharp rocks, but their large size facilitates travel across expanses of soft mud. In water they serve as swimming paddles and are the chief means of propulsion. A most unusual feature is the split claw on the second toe of the hind foot, which is used to clean and comb out the fur to prevent it from matting and from losing its waterproofing and insulating characteristics.

The front legs are not used for swimming, but on land, they serve their owner well in a multitude of ways. The feet have five toes, and there is a heavy growth of hairs on their backs. The palms are naked and covered with a tough, black epidermis. The fingers have only rudimentary webs between them and are furnished with strong claws, which function as very efficient digging tools. On land they are very important in locomotion, but in the water they are pressed closely against the side of the body. It is sometimes said that the beaver swims with his hands tucked into his vest pockets.

The front feet are used to lift and carry objects, even some that are very heavy. Beavers carry mud and other objects "in their arms" and hold them close to the body, tucked under the chin. Solid objects are pushed into place with either the teeth, the front legs, or both. Mud is dug up,

19

A subadult beaver just out of the pond with wet fur. The front feet with their sharp claws can be clearly seen as well as the muscular tail stalk.

carried, and pushed into place with the front feet. Sometimes he also uses his forehead to press mud or earth in place, very much in the manner of a squirrel burying a nut.

The beaver is very dextrous in the use of its front feet. With them he can manipulate objects with a high degree of skill. This is especially evident to anyone who has had the good fortune to witness the "corn-on-the-cob" eating technique of a beaver peeling and eating the bark from a piece of wood. He cuts a stick to a convenient length, peels it, and discards it in a short period of time. Then he repeats the process with a new stick. On land, the beaver reminds one of a squirrel in many of its poses and actions, especially when it is eating. However, while the squirrel holds its tail upright, the beaver's will be flat on the ground serving as a prop.

Tail

The broad canoe-paddle-shaped tail of the beaver is his special trademark. Because of it he is one of the most widely recognized of all animals. The broad part or blade is attached to the body by a heavily muscled stalk which is completely covered with hair. The length and

This four to six-year-old beaver is in summer fur and probably weighs well in excess of fifty pounds. The top of the broad flat tail can be clearly seen.

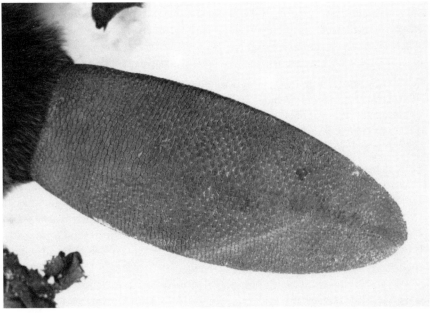

This closeup dorsal view of the tail appears scaled, but these are not true scales.

width of the tail varies among individuals. In Wyoming, Grasse and Putnam (6) made some comparisons among beavers that they had live trapped. They measured a number of individuals, but the maximum and minimum are as follows.

Weight	Total Length	Tail Length	Tail Width
60 lb	45 inches	12 inches	7.5 inches
23 lb	37 inches	10 inches	4.5 inches

The tail is shiny black in color and appears to be covered with scales on both top and lower surfaces. Those on top are larger in diameter. These, however, are not true scales, but are instead simply dips or depressions in the tough skin of the tail. Morgan stated that it contains a large amount of fatty tissue. This would suggest that it can store up fat to provide a reserve supply of energy in time of scarcity of food.

Bradt (4) claimed that the beaver feels little pain even when a branding iron is pressed against its tail. In Michigan, an attempt was made to identify beavers that were captured and released by putting brands on their tails. Because of shedding or sloughing away of the scaly surface, the brands became obscure, and the process was discontinued.

The tail serves its owner well in a number of ways. It acts as a prop to help the beaver sit or stand erect. When walking on its hind legs, the beaver achieves greater stability by using its tail. It also gives added leverage when the beaver is cutting down a tree or lifting or carrying heavy objects. Sometimes when the beaver is sitting, the tail sticks out behind, but it may also be tucked under the body and used as a seat. When the beaver is sleeping, it may be tucked against the side of the body like that of a cat. Enos Mills (13) commented,

> I have seen a beaver carry a small dab of mud or some sticks clasped between the tail and the body. This gives an awkward animal an increased awkwardness and even an uncouth appearance to see him humped up with its tail tucked between its legs to clasp something between it and the body.

In sharp contrast with its awkward movements on land, the beaver is completely at home in the water. It swims, floats, and dives with effortless ease, and it swims equally well whether on the surface or submerged. With head held high and ears erect, it spends long periods of time swimming, seemingly for the sheer enjoyment that it affords. When swimming on the surface, the beaver propels itself by alternate strokes of its huge, webbed hind feet.

The tail serves as a steering and diving rudder. When the beaver swims under water, the tail also becomes a most important organ of locomotion. It functions as a sculling oar, but it usually moves up and

Top: The beaver has just struck the water with his tail but continues to swim. This kind of slap is often repeated numerous times with a KA-PLUNK sound and expresses resentment at an intruder. The first part of the sound is made when the tail is raised and the second when it strikes the water. Middle: The tail is raised to maximum height ready to be brought down with such force that it makes a hole in the water and a sound like a pistol shot. The beaver then disappears in a power dive. This is definitely a warning sign. Bottom: Splash made by the tail at the moment of impact.

down like the flippers of dolphins or the flukes of whales rather than from side to side like the tail of a fish. It can also be turned and moved from side to side.

Although the beaver swims with consummate ease, either on the surface or under water, there are other animals that swim faster and are far more agile. The otter, for example, can overtake, outmaneuver and capture fish. This the beaver cannot do.

There are times when an intruder, human or otherwise, appears at a pond at which time a wary beaver may lie or cruise semi-submerged, showing only a small triangle—the tip of the nose, eyes, ears and the top of the head—above the water's surface. With only this tiny portion of its body exposed, it can fully appraise the situation. If danger appears to threaten, it may do one of two things: either submerge quietly and seek a place of safety or sound a warning by striking the water with the tail with such force that there is a resounding splash with a sound as sharp and piercing as a pistol shot that can be heard three-quarters of a mile away.

This unusual action is peculiar to the beaver. It may be done suddenly and without warning, or before it happens, the tail may be held in a cocked position in which it is slightly raised in the middle. It may be held in that position for several moments. When the slap is executed, the tail may be flipped straight up and brought down with such force that it makes a hole in the water, sends up a shower of spray, and forces the beaver into a power dive. This happens so fast that a 1/500th of a second camera shutter speed cannot stop the action except when the tail is at its maximum height, just before it begins its downward swing. The muscles that lower the tail are much stronger than those that raise it.

There are times when beavers slap the water with their tails without diving. This typically occurs when an intruder is present. They frequently swim in circles around a boat or canoe, dive, and surface again without making a sound. At other times, a beaver may raise its tail slightly and then flip it down with a gentle slap that makes a peculiar "K—plunk" sound.

It is generally believed that the sound made by slapping the water with the tail is a signal to all beavers within hearing to take cover and seek safety, but this is not always the case. In some instances other members of the family will continue eating in spite of warning splashes. One thing is certain, however: the slapping of the tail is a sign that the beaver resents the presence of the creature that is trespassing in its domain.

Metabolism

The beaver's metabolism proceeds at a slower rate than does that of more active creatures of comparable size, especially those that must be active during the rigorous conditions of northern winters. Therefore, muscular energy is released and used at a slower rate, and the rate of respiration is also slower. Less oxygen is used to maintain body heat because when the ponds are covered with ice, the beaver seldom strays far from the pond. There, in the house or in the water, temperatures never are below freezing, and the animal's waterproof fur coat and the insulating layers of fat under its skin constitute a most efficient combination to prevent the loss of heat.

While there may be occasions when the beaver is on the land that its inability to release and utilize muscular energy at a rapid rate for sustained periods of time may be critical to survival, in the water the beaver's slow rate of respiration is distinctly to its advantage. Also contributing to the beaver's ability to remain under water for extended periods of time are its unusually large liver and lungs. Both serve as reservoirs for storing oxygenated blood, and the lungs are capable of a very efficient oxygen-to-carbon-dioxide exchange rate of seventy-five per cent, as compared to between fifteen and twenty per cent for human lung efficiency (1). Under ordinary conditions a beaver can swim for a quarter of a mile under water without coming up for air, and under unusual conditions it can remain under water up to fifteen minutes.

In addition to its ability to stay under water for prolonged periods without coming up for air, the beaver has developed a special technique for rebreathing air. When travelling under the ice, it can rise to the surface and carefully expel a large bubble of stale air which spreads out under the ice. This must be done with precise accuracy to prevent it from breaking up into small bubbles. At a later time, after the bubble has exchanged its load of carbon dioxide for a fresh supply of oxygen, the beaver can return and carefully rebreathe the air. Under normal conditions, this is a convenience rather than a necessity because the beaver can always swim to its house or a bank burrow where it can come up for air. There may also be holes in the ice at the edge of a pond where members of the family can come out and make short excursions on the land.

Food Sources and Habits

Some observers in different locations have made meticulous records of the items that beavers eat, but I found that this can well be an exercise in futility. The only limiting factor in a beaver's diet is the fact that it is a strict vegetarian. Other than that, there seems to be nothing

Subadult and adult beaver. The young one is eating an apple. Its fur is wet, and the full tail, including the muscular tail stalk, can be clearly seen.

in the form of plant life available that it will not eat and cannot digest. That includes a number of species that are poisonous to other forms of animals and to humans. No tree is too hard, too bitter, or too gummy for the beaver to cut down, cut up, and utilize, nor will even the size of a tree faze it. This fact was demonstrated beyond a shadow of a doubt in Grand Tetons National Park in Wyoming. There, near the Snake River, beavers cut down a number of cottonwood trees. The largest had a stump diameter of over three and a half feet. In the same vicinity lay the trunks of several others of slightly lesser size.

"Old Bark Burner" is one of the names that the beaver has been called. In large measure it is most appropriate because the beaver does consume vast quantities of bark, especially in winter when it is the only food available in large quantities. Even then, the animal varies its diet with roots when it can find them. During the spring and summer, most of the cutting done by beavers is for the purpose of acquiring building materials and for simply keeping its teeth worn down and honed to razor sharpness. Of the sticks it cuts, it peels and eats the bark from some, but others are used as building materials without peeling. During the growing season, beavers feed freely upon anything that

26

grows in the water, on the surface, and at the edges. Out on the land beavers dine with gusto on grasses, forbs, leaves, mushrooms, fruits, and berries. In places where they are available, beavers have sometimes developed a special fondness for apples, a fondness that is not always appreciated by the owners of apple trees. If a beaver gets impatient for the fruit to fall, it cuts down the trees.

By mid-summer, it may be difficult to see the surface of a small natural or man-made pond because the surface is completely covered with Duckweed, Bladderwort, and other floating water plants. Beneath the surface the water may be choked with a rank growth of eel grass, elodea, and milfoil. A new beaver pond, for a time, may have a similar appearance because the plants grow faster than a pair of beavers can eat them, but when the family grows larger, anything that grows on or in the pond is freely eaten, especially the Duckweed. A beaver will slowly swim along the surface of the water, suck in the duckweed, and eat it, sometimes using its front feet to concentrate it and sweep it into its mouth. The members of the beaver family will also have ample help from the immigrating muskrats and waterfowl in disposing of any water plants that grow in the ponds, once the beavers have moved in and begun their work. Muskrats consume duckweed in the same manner as the beavers. Ultimately, a well-established beaver pond will have very little water vegetation. For the most part, it is consumed as fast as it grows, the one exception in ponds of long standing being water lilies—usually yellow lilies or spatterdock, but sometimes also tuberous water lilies, sweet-scented water lilies, or any combination of the three.

Teeth

Its large chisel-like front teeth rank a very close second to its tail as the beaver's special trademark. They are also its chief working tools, and they serve their owner exceedingly well in a multitude of ways. There are four of these great incisors: two grow from the front of the upper jaw, two from the lower. The upper set extends out from the jaw about one inch, the lower approximately an inch and three quarters, and the upper set overlaps the lower. In an average-sized beaver, the teeth are about a quarter of an inch in width and in thickness. Very large animals have correspondingly larger teeth.

The front surface of the incisors is covered with a thin, orange-colored layer of extremely hard enamel which is backed by a softer layer of dentine. This wears down quickly when the beaver bites on hard objects, and a sharp cutting edge is formed with a bevel about the same as the cutting edge of a carpenter's chisel. The teeth are self-sharpening, self-repairing, and continue to grow as long as the owner lives. When beavers chew under water, their lips can close in behind their teeth to prevent water from getting into their throats.

Front view showing incisor teeth. The beaver can use its teeth underwater because it can close its lips behind the incisors and thus prevent water from getting into the throat. The incisors are extremely efficient cutting tools and are powered by jaw muscles so massive that the animal seems to have an acute case of mumps.

An adult beaver skull showing the massive jaw bones needed for the teeth to be used as cutting tools. An adult beaver has twenty teeth: two incisors and eight molars in the upper jaw and two incisors and eight molars in the lower jaw. At the back of the skull is the opening through which the auditory nerve enters the brain.

28

In addition to the usual ways in which teeth serve their owners, the incisors perform the same operations that the tools of the lumberjack and logger perform. They serve as axe, saw peavy, canthook, and pike pole. With them the beaver cuts down trees, trims them, and cuts the logs into lengths. This done, it rolls or drags them to the desired positions. In the water the teeth are used to grasp a pole or length of log, tow it where the beaver wishes to use it, and place it in the position desired.

When a beaver is peeling a stick, it holds the stick with its front feet and as it turns it over, the teeth operate like a lathe chisel. This cutting is done nearly as fast as a human could accomplish the same action using a lathe. In all these operations the beaver's teeth are operated and controlled by powerful sets of jaw muscles so massive that they give to the beaver's head the appearance of a creature with a very severe case of mumps.

Blue Beech, Water Beech, Musclewood are three of the names by which this tree is known. Because of its hardness, it is also known as Ironwood. There is no tree so hard, so bitter, or so gummy that beavers will not cut and eat it. Where aspens, cottonwoods, and Blue Beech are equally available, beavers often prefer this to other species. The trunk nearer the water was girdled and killed at an earlier time.

29

It is common belief that the beaver fells a tree by gnawing around the base until it falls, but in reality it uses a far faster and more efficient method, enabling it to cut down a tree about as fast as an average person could do it with an axe. The beaver approaches a selected tree, makes several deep bites into it, and then repeats the process several inches above or below the first cuts. This done, it takes a firm grip between cuts, twists out a chip, drops it, and repeats the operation. This is usually done from a sitting position with the tail serving as a prop. If the tree is of small diameter, up to six inches at the stump, the beaver may never change its position. When cutting a larger tree, the animal works on it at different times and usually works around it until it falls.

A beaver cut these two poplar trees rapidly and from only one side. The size of the chips in the pile attest to the sharpness of the teeth and the power of the jaw muscles.

A chip is taken out in a matter of seconds. Many are an inch in width and in thickness and up to six inches in length. Unlike the skilled lumberjack who can determine the direction that a tree will fall, a beaver-cut tree falls in the direction that it naturally leans. Many

30

Beavers are often wasteful in their cutting. When a tree lodges in the tops of others, no effort is made to fell it. Unless it is blown down by the wind or the trees holding it up happen to also get cut, the tree is wasted.

beaver-cut trees lodge in the tops of others and are thus wasted since beavers make no further effort to bring them down. There are also well-documented instances where beavers have been crushed and killed when the trees they cut down fell on them.

Four poplars felled by beavers. Contrary to the belief held by many, the beaver cannot determine the direction in which a tree will fall. When it is cut, a tree falls in the direction that it naturally leans. Here the beavers cut four trees and each fell in a different direction. The trunks of trees of this diameter are seldom cut up and used, but the branches have been trimmed and dragged away.

The number of trees cut down in any locality where beavers live depends upon a number of factors: the size and number of those doing the cutting, the length of time that the area has been occupied, the size and abundance of the trees growing in the immediate vicinity, and the distance they stand from the water. As a rule, there is more cutting when beavers first move into an area. In addition to the brush and trees cut for food, there is a heavy demand for sticks, poles, and lengths of logs to build dams and construct houses.

Subsequently, the intensity of cutting activity varies with the season of the year, and the greatest amount of cutting occurs when beavers prepare the pond for winter. It is then that dams must be made secure and houses made into snug living quarters. Of special importance is an adequate food supply for the long months when the pond may be locked in ice and covered with snow from November until mid-April.

Food Storage

Beavers begin storing food for winter in a leisurely manner several weeks before cold weather arrives, often in early September. First, they tow a few pieces of brush to the vicinity of the main entrance to the lodge or burrow. They push these down into the mud, and from that time on, they add more material to the pile and pack it down into a compact mass. Every day sees the pile growing bigger as trip after trip is made onto the land to cut and secure more material. As the season progresses, the action goes on at a rapidly increasing pace until a peak of activity is reached by the time the leaves take on their autumn colors. An occasional early fall of snow does not hinder the beavers in these activities, but as soon as a layer of ice forms on the water, the work comes to an abrupt halt.

Beaver house and partially stocked foodpile being readied for winter.

There has been considerable speculation concerning the method by which the material in the food pile is submerged and why it does not float. It has been claimed that beavers suck the air out of each stick to make it sink. This, of course, is preposterous and also an impossibility. In actual practice, the beavers may push the ends of the first layers firmly into the mud to hold them down, and successive layers are piled on top and pressed down. As more and more new material is added to the pile, the sheer weight holds down the lower layers. Then too, the material is cut green and is thus full of sap, and after it has been submerged for a time, it becomes completely waterlogged. Even so, parts of the top layer will be visible above the surface of the water.

Depending upon the locality and the trees that grow there, there may be wide variation in the diameters of the material stored in the

Beavers will eat the bark from larger diameter trees with smooth bark, such as the birch shown, than from trees with rough bark.

food pile. Where smooth-bark trees predominate, beavers cut and use much larger sections than where trees with rough bark must be used.

It is true that work on storing food stops when the water freezes over. However, spring never seems to arrive soon enough, and there are times in the middle of the winter when beaver break out from under the ice and make forays onto land to cut fresh food. A number of years ago, hikers on their way to the summit of Mount Marcy, the highest peak in the Adirondack Mountains of New York State, could well have observed some most interesting beaver work. A considerable number of Yellow Birch trees had been cut along the shore of Avalanche Lake. They had fallen into the water, and a number had been trimmed. This in itself is not unusual for Yellow Birch bark, twigs, leaves, and buds are favorite beaver food. Higher up on the bank on the other side of the trail, however, there were several stumps about six inches in diameter that stood at least five feet above the ground. Curious observers must have wondered how beavers did the cutting so high above the ground. The only possible explanation is that the beaver doing the cutting was standing on a snow bank.

From a series of studies conducted concerning beaver behavior in Michigan, we acquire some reliable information concerning the number of trees that will be cut down per beaver, the percentage that is utilized of each tree cut, and the carrying capacity of an area that is occupied by beavers. Bradt (4) reported in 1947 that at Michigan State College six captive adult beavers collectively consumed one hundred eighty, one-inch to three-inch poplars in a month for an average of approximately one tree per beaver per day, or three hundred sixty-five trees per beaver in a year. This study did not account for the other types of food that beavers eat, which are plentiful during the summer season.

From a careful count of stumps of trees that beavers had cut in two game management areas in Michigan, Bradt (4) concluded that an adult beaver will cut an average of 0.592 or 0.6 trees per day. He found that most of the cutting was done within two hundred feet of the lake, but he mentions instances in which beavers had dragged poplars for measured distances of six hundred fifty feet.

On the basis of his observations he concluded that an acre of poplars two inches in diameter with a density of fifteen hundred trees per acre will support one beaver for seven years or seven beavers for one year, and an acre of poplars of the same size with a population density of three thousand trees per acre will support one beaver for fourteen years or fourteen beavers for one year. These figures do not take into account the rate of growth of trees, but in any event it is most unusual for a family of beavers to occupy any area for fourteen years. Long before that time, they have usually cut down and used up the trees that stood at convenient distances from the water. From other studies of the food habits of beavers, results have indicated that over eighty per cent of a two-inch poplar cut for food is utilized (4). Grasse and Putnam (6) reported that in Wyoming, beavers utilize eighty-eight per cent of a two-inch poplar, fifty per cent of a three-inch poplar, and thirty-four per cent of a four-inch poplar.

This animal has displayed an amazing ability to adapt its behavior according to local conditions. This applies to the storing of food for the winter. However, Kenneth C. Smith (17) has reported, "With Louisiana's mild winters there is no need to stockpile food. It is there for the taking all year long. There is no necessity for felling large numbers of trees and saplings to store in the water."

Few, if any, of the creatures that walk on four legs have digestive systems that begin to match the efficiency of that of the beaver. In its ability to consume and utilize low-grade foods, the beaver is in a class by itself. Because many of the things it eats are of low nutritional

Trees the size of these poplar saplings are easily felled, cut up, carried away and stored in the food pile. All of the bark can be eaten and there is very little wasteful cutting of trees this size.

quality, it must consume them in great quantities. The price it pays for this advantage is that it must carry around an immense digestive system and its heavy load of contents. This accounts for its slow and sometimes clumsy movements when it is on land.

Digestion

Digestion begins with the cutting up of food with its great incisors. From them the material is passed back to a set of grinding teeth. These are the molars, sixteen in all, arranged in sets of four, with eight in the lower jaw and eight in the upper. They move not only in the usual manner, from side to side, but forward and backward as well, grinding the food into very fine particles. After the food is swallowed, it enters a digestive system that is especially developed to process it.

In their report of beaver studies in Maine, Hodgdon and Hunt (11) provided the following information.

> In the beaver the upper end of the stomach has a secretory gland that is greatly developed. The thickening of the stomach wall where this gland is located is pronounced. There are 8 openings into the stomach, each about 1/2 the size of a pencil. It is presumed

35

that the high development of this gland is related to the beaver's use of woody material as a food.

Indeed this gland produces an enzyme which reduces some of the cellulose to starch, which is then subject to further reduction by other agents to digestible sugar. In addition to this secretory gland, the beaver's digestive system includes a large "great colon" and a very large caecum. Large as it is, however, it is not out of proportion to the caeca of other rodents or the lagomorphs (rabbits and hares) (1).

The beaver is a very clean animal in its personal habits. Elimination of wastes takes place at a distance from its house, usually under water and in the vicinity of the dam. Because of the quantities of woody material that are consumed and eliminated under water, a pond bottom soon becomes carpeted with a layer of finely shredded wood fibers.

On the basis of Bradt's conclusion that an acre of two-inch diameter saplings will support one beaver for seven years or seven beavers for one year, it is interesting to speculate on the quantity of wood fibers that would accumulate on a pond bottom after a number of years of occupancy, but it is also impossible to compute with any degree of accuracy the quantity of that accumulation. First, under normal conditions, beavers consume vast quantities of plant materials containing woody fibers in addition to what they get from trees, and it is impossible to determine the volume of material in the form of peeled sticks that are piled on the top of the house or carried over the dam. In any event, where a pond has been continuously occupied by a family of eight or ten beavers for a period of several years, that accumulation would amount to a volume of several cords of wood, each measuring 4 x 4 x 8 feet or 128 cubic feet. In addition, mixed with it would be the accumulation of silt that had settled out from mud carried downstream during periods of high water.

Reproduction and Family Life

Except during the late stages of pregnancy or when a female is nursing young, it is not possible to determine the sex of a beaver from external appearances. The external genitalia are identical in both sexes. However, the oil from the torpedo-shaped oil glands, located near the anal opening, is sometimes observable externally, and it differs between males and females. Allred reports that in the female the oil is pale yellow and light in viscosity while that of the male is very viscous and coppery brown. This oil is used to waterproof the beaver's fur.

Records from both Michigan and Maine indicate that the peak of the breeding season occurs during the middle two weeks of February, but it varies with geographic latitude, altitude, and with the ages of the parent beavers. The gestation period averages approximately one hundred ten days, and specific birth times appear to coincide with the arrival of spring weather in a particular thermal line (1). There are exceptions, however. This was demonstrated most dramatically at Bullhead Pond, a small natural pond located east of Watertown, New York, close to the border of the Adirondack State Park. The purpose of the trip there was to tape-record the voices of the beavers that lived inside a very large house at the side of the lake. While this was in progress, I saw what appeared to be a muskrat on the side of the house at the water's edge. On closer inspection it proved to be a very small beaver. It is unusual to see a kit that small alone outside the house at any season, but it was extraordinary to see such a thing in late October.

Grasse and Putnam (6) reported that a kit beaver trapped on November 15, 1949, weighed four pounds fourteen ounces, and they estimated that it had been born no earlier than the first of September.

When young are about to be born, the male beaver moves out and lives apart from his family until the young are well developed. During that time he lives the life of a typical bachelor beaver. He may take up residence in a den half a mile or more from his family, but he does make frequent trips back to the pond to make repairs and additions to the dam.

The one-hundred-ten-day gestation is an unusually long period of time for a rodent, but as a result the young are born well-developed. At birth they weigh about one pound each, their eyes are open, their teeth are well-developed, and they are fully furred. They can walk the day they are born and can swim soon thereafter. Litters typically number from two to four, but litters of eight have been reported. The female can nurse four kits at a time. There are two teats between the front legs and two farther back on the body.

Young beavers grow rapidly. Vernon Bailey has reported that at three weeks, beaver kits weigh from one-and-a-half to two pounds, and at six weeks four pounds (3). Studies in Maine revealed that by December, the average weight of kits was fifteen pounds and by the following spring, it had increased to seventeen pounds (3). If a human infant grew at the same rate as a baby beaver, at the age of six months it would weigh between ninety and one hundred twenty pounds. The young begin to eat the leafy material the female brings them when they are two to three weeks of age, but continue to nurse for five or six weeks (1). At the age of one month, they begin eating solid food, and at six weeks they are fully weaned.

This beaver kit weighed approximately fifteen pounds in September. When it was born in May, it weighed only one pound.

A night photograph of an adult beaver with kit, taken in October. The kit weighs about fifteen pounds and the adult between thirty and forty.

An almost certain sign that there are young in the house is the sight of an adult beaver swimming toward it with a mouthful of brush or grasses. As the young get older, these trips become more frequent. More evidence that there are young inside are the insistent sounds of hungry young begging for food that can frequently be heard coming from the house. Although young beavers can swim soon after they are born, they are typically kept inside the house until they are well able to take care of themselves. Because young beavers are light, they float like corks and cannot dive, which renders them easy prey for eagles, large hawks, or Great Horned Owls.

The young do very little useful work during their first summer, and it is doubtful that they could survive their first winter without their parents. Because of the protection given to the young when they are most vulnerable to predators, the rate of survival is very high in places where they are not molested by man.

By the end of November, subadults have attained a weight of twenty-five pounds but during the winter they put on little additional weight. Bailey (3) found the average weights of adults to be from thirty to fifty pounds, but that a fifty-pound animal was a very rare individual. He also recorded a few older animals that weighed from sixty to one hundred pounds.

Young beavers stay with the family until after their second winter. When they leave they are well able to live independent lives. Beavers in captivity have been known to live seventeen years, with an average life span of about fifteen (1). Enos Mills (13) observed one, Old Flat Top, over a period of eighteen years, and because the beaver was probably four years old when it was first observed, it may have been twenty-two years old.

Interactions between adult beavers and their young can provide the observer with considerable amusement and cause for speculation. On Red House Lake in Allegany State Park near Salamanca, New York, I once watched an adult swimming in the lake with a small kit riding on its back. From time to time, the adult would dive, leaving the young one paddling furiously. A short time later, the big one would come up under the young one, and it would ride on the back again. Whether this was a form of play or a swimming lesson or a combination thereof is a matter of conjecture.

Musk Bogs and Sign Heaps

Around beaver ponds there are special areas that are referred to as musk bogs. These are places where entire families sometimes climb out of the pond, void their musk, roll in the grass , and then they usually sit down and begin the process of combing out, cleaning and oiling their fur. When that is done, the larger ones may rest or sleep. At such times the little ones may wrestle, push one another into the water and engage

Subadult beaver. The front feet are not used in swimming, but are used almost like human hands for digging, moving sticks and stones and for cleaning the fur.

in other forms of play. It is through play that they develop their muscles and learn some of the things that they will need to survive later on.

Among the many distinctive things he does, the beaver "makes mud pies." These are constructed very much in the manner of those made by many generations of country children. After a rain they often amuse themselves by playing in the mud, which often involves digging up the mud with their hands, piling it up, spreading it out, and patting it down. This is precisely the method used by the beaver and with end results strikingly similar in appearance and dimensions, but there is one difference. When a beaver completes his work, he signs it. This he does by placing on it a few drops of musk from castor glands at the base of the tail. This secretion is known as castoreum.

These mud pies are technically known as sign heaps, and whenever a wandering beaver comes across one, it literally gets the message that beavers are in residence in this area. When mud is not available, the beaver uses whatever material is at hand. I have personally seen sign heaps composed of rotted leaves dug up from the bottom of the pond and sign heaps made from sphagnum moss. On one occasion I saw sphagnum piled on the end of a piece of wood that stuck out from the bank along the side of a canal. The beaver is not the only territorial animal that marks the boundaries of the area he claims, but his method is distinctive. These sign heaps not only warn off trespassers, but they could well be used by a bachelor beaver to advertise for a mate.

Castors have commercial value when properly dried. They are used in medicines, animal scents, and as a fixative in perfume. Their most important use at the present time is in the making of high quality perfumes (6).

Grasse and Putnam (6) noted the following with regard to live-trapping beavers.

> Several ingredients of beaver scent are intended to appeal to the beaver's appetite, but the basic ingredient, beaver castors, makes him want to investigate the presence of strange beaver. Males, at least, are definitely on the fight at the first smell of beaver scent. The hair on their backs raise, and they hiss and blow in a grand show of beaver anger. Beaver, too, are much like dogs in that everywhere that one beaver has been, every other beaver that

A recently constructed mud pie or sign heap. It will mark the beaver's territory when given a few drops of castoreum from its musk glands. Mud is usually used for construction as this one is, but sphagnum moss or other materials are sometimes used.

41

comes along must go also. Scent is very valuable to us in live trapping.

Getting the beaver into the live-trap does not end the operation. He must then be transferred to a holding pen to wait until a suitable mate can be secured to accompany him when he is finally released.

A beaver's reaction to scent is interesting to watch. His first reaction is usually a grand show of beaver anger. The hair on his back rises and he hisses and swims around, apparently trying to locate an intruder. Quite often he will charge the exact spot where the scent has been placed and go right into the trap. If he misses the trap he will climb out onto the bank, scratch around the scented spot, and then pile mud and sticks on it. The scented spot becomes the center of his activity for some time. On several occasions we have watched a beaver go back and forth over a supposedly well set trap several times before he finally stepped on the pan.

Beavers are subject to relatively few diseases. In a large measure this is the result of living in tightly knit family units with little or no contact with others of their kind. Thus, even if a contagious disease strikes one family, it is not transmitted to others. There is little danger of beavers being stricken with the types of plague that sometimes wipes out entire populations of large prairie-dog towns.

After their second winter, the two-year-olds are forcibly driven from the family group, making room for the young that are about to be born. It prolongs the time a family may stay in its domain before the food supply is exhausted, and it is nature's way of preventing inbreeding. The exodus usually takes place in March, and during that month beavers can sometimes be found in unusual places. At dawn one March day, a beaver was found wandering down the main street of the village of Monticello, New York. On another March day, a beaver was spotted on a pile of driftwood at the upper side of the Main Street Bridge of the City of Rochester, New York. Beavers are strongly territorial, and any young beaver wandering into the domain of a family will be forcibly driven out. These wanderings to seek new territory may be relatively short trips up or down stream to a place that seems to be suitable and unoccupied, but some wandering beavers have been found as far away as twenty-nine miles from the pond where they were born (11). It is during such times that individuals are in the greatest danger from predators.

When a wandering beaver arrives at a location that is not occupied by other beavers, if the place seems suited to its needs, and if the beaver decides to settle there, it stakes out its claim to this territory in that peculiar manner described above, by making mud pies and signing them with musk from the castor glands. Thus it has marked its territory, warned off rivals, and put out a sign to attract a mate all at once.

A beaver living alone is referred to as a bachelor. It may be of either sex or any age, but usually it is either a young one that has been driven out from the family group or an old one without a family. These solitary beavers usually do little work. They live in dens dug into banks or possibly an abandoned house.

Predators

The beaver is a relatively large animal that is not well-adapted to living on the land. Water protects it from predators, but the beaver needs to get in and out of its house or den at all seasons, especially in the northern part of its range where ice may be eighteen inches or more in thickness. The beaver is seldom locked in its house or is frozen out as sometimes happens with muskrats when unusually cold winters freeze marshes to the bottom. This is a result of the beaver locating its house in the area of a spring as well as its digging up mud to plaster the house in preparation for winter. The deepest part of the pond is typically at the mouths of the tunnels that serve as the doors to the living quarters.

Except for man, the beaver is well-equipped to cope with the presence of predators. It is safest in winter when it is in snug dens protected by thick layers of ice, out of sight and out of reach. Among the predators that pursue beavers are the Grizzly Bear, the Black Bear, the Cougar, the Lynx, the Bobcat, the Wolf, the Coyote, the Wolverine, and the Fisher. In the most unusual event that a very young beaver would be found unattended, we might add to the list foxes, Gray Owls, Great Horned Owls, Red-tailed Hawks, and eagles. Today, several of these predators are themselves high on the list of endangered species. Under man's protection, on the other hand, the beaver is making a strong comeback.

In the water there are two possible predators to consider: the alligator and the otter. Warm climate alone does not prohibit the beaver from extending its range southward. In Big Bend National Park, there are beavers living on both the American and Mexican sides of the river. There the Rio Grande flows through a desert where temperatures often reach 120 degrees Fahrenheit. On the other hand, in Okefenokee Swamp in South Georgia, there are no beavers. There the chance of a beaver living to a ripe old age would be very slim as it would have little chance to protect itself from a twelve-foot-long alligator.

When one considers the predator-prey relationship between the Lynx and the Snowshoe Hare, the Fisher and the Porcupine, the Marten and the Red Squirrel, the Black-footed Ferret and the Prairie Dog, and especially the Mink and the Muskrat, it is interesting to speculate upon the possible predator-prey relationship between the otter and the beaver. Except for size, in many ways the lifestyle and behavior of the mink is very similar to that of the otter, and those of the

43

A pair of Bald Eagles built a nest in a large, dead, Cottonwood tree that stood in the middle of a former Beaver pond along the Snake River in Grand Tetons National Park. Fortunately for any Beavers living in the vicinity, Bald Eagles feed chiefly on fish. However, Golden Eagles regularly prey upon animals the size of young lambs of Antelope and Big Horn Sheep. Young Beavers would be easy prey for them.

Bark is an important part of the diet of both the beaver and the porcupine. However, unlike the beaver, the porcupine lives in the treetops and eats the bark directly from the limbs.

44

muskrat very similar to those of the beaver. The otter is a superb swimmer, can easily outmaneuver a beaver in the water, and is the only potential predator that can enter a beaver house from the water at any season of the year.

Grey Owl (8) stated that he found beaver fur in the droppings of a marauding otter. This raises the question of whether the otter did the killing or took advantage of the kill of another predator. I received some interesting replies to letters I wrote to the game departments of forty-eight states and those of Canada concerning this question. In most instances it appears that there usually is no conflict, and some cited instances where beavers and otters lived together in the same ponds. However, it was the opinion of some of those contacted that under certain conditions, otters might prey upon very young beavers.

Mr. J. A. Trembly, Director of Fur Service, of the Department of Fish and Game, Province of Quebec, answered my question of how do beavers and otters get along as follows. "Not so well, according to our records. This winter, on the North Shore of the St. Laurence River, a family of beavers and one dead otter were found in a beaver house after a fight." Ernest Thompson Seaton reported that he saw a family of beavers drive an otter out of the pond. John Mathias, an Algonquin guide and expert trapper who lived at Rapides des Joachims, P. Q., reported that he saw a family of beavers kill an otter.

Leo A. Luttringer, Jr., former editor of *Pennsylvania Game News,* wrote that Mr. Harry Van Cleve, veteran trapper of The Game Commission, had on two occasions pulled dead otters from beaver dams. From the cuts and scratches on their bodies, it appeared that "they [had] suffered cruelly at the hands of the beavers." However, Mr. Luttringer continued on another note, "On June 12, 1930, Game Protector George H. Watrous found two otters living in the same pond with the beaver colony. The place is known as Page's Pond in Susquehanna County." Since that writing the otter was declared to be extinct in Pennsylvania, but it is now just beginning to become re-established there.

In most of the northeastern states, the otter is a very rare animal and poses no threat to the beaver population. Conflicts between the two appear to be very rare. Even though the otter is more agile and can easily outmaneuver a beaver either on land or in the water, the advantage is with the beaver. The teeth of the otter are short, but those of the beaver are long and sharp. In addition, the beaver has a thick coat of fur and under it, a very tough hide. Moreover, reports indicate that one otter may be fighting against two or more beavers at the same time.

During the winter months, the beaver is out of reach of predators, but it is not an easy prey at any season. It is strong and capable of dragging a lynx or bobcat that may be riding on its back into the water with him. There are numerous reports of conflicts between dogs and beavers, and in most cases the dogs were heavy losers. There is one authenticated report of a farm dog with the reputation of being "death to woodchucks" that caught a large beaver away from the water. A terrific fight ensued, and when it was over, the dog was badly mauled and cut up whereas the beaver suffered little damage.

The wide range that the beaver occupied and the numbers of individual beavers within that range are ample proof that the beaver is well able to survive in the presence of its natural enemies. Today, the Grizzly, Wolverine, Cougar, Fisher, and wolves no longer exist in the areas now occupied by the beaver. Of all its potential natural enemies, only the coyote has been steadily extending its range.

Bull elk, with antlers in velvet, grazing in a beaver meadow of Yellowstone National Park in early spring.

Competitors

There are situations where competitors are a more serious threat to the welfare of beavers than their predators. This has been dramatically demonstrated in Yellowstone National Park. At the time President Grant signed the proclamation creating the park, it was off limits to hunters and trappers, and as a result beavers thrived and multiplied. For a number of years one of the chief tourist attractions was the opportunity to watch beavers at work. As a result there are a number of ponds and beaver meadows, many covering areas of from forty to fifty acres or more. Evidence of the former abundance is everywhere, but the beaver became a scarce animal within the park. The reason: the overabundance of elk. As long as there were trees to cut down within convenient distances from the water, the beavers had no problem. When they were gone, the elk browsed off any seedlings that reared their heads. On Signal Mountain there was a beaver pond where the only trees available were Lodgepole Pines. In this location their chief foods were grasses and pond lilies.

Intelligence

To what degree the works of the beaver are accomplished by a dumb creature programmed to respond to its environment solely by instinct or to what extent they have been performed by a creature of considerable intelligence, or a combination of the two, raises questions to which there are no positive answers. Any opinion expressed on the subject is a matter of conjecture.

Rodents are not generally considered to be creatures that possess a high degree of intelligence. Nevertheless, the beaver has repeatedly demonstrated that it can learn from experience, that it can remember, and that it can solve problems. It also has repeatedly demonstrated that once it starts a course of action, it is well nigh impossible for a human to deter it short of removing it or killing it. There are times when it appears to display a sardonic sense of humor in thwarting man's attempts to circumvent it. Dozens of instances could be cited to illustrate this point, but perhaps the following will suffice.

A few years ago Camp Massaweepie, the summer camp of the Rochester Area Council Boy Scouts of America at Gale, New York, had a beaver problem. Beavers decided to build a dam close to the camp headquarters building. Every day campers tore the dam out, and every night the beavers built it up. This went on until someone who had heard that beavers shun anything that carries human odor decided to take action. Above the break they hung an old pair of dungarees that had been much worn and saturated with human odor. For two nights the beavers shunned the place, but on the third they pulled them down and buried them in the dam.

In the museum at Rocky Mountain National Park, Estes Park, Colorado, is an exhibit that is most convincing proof that a beaver can be a very difficult creature to discourage. In an effort to prevent a beaver from cutting down a small cottonwood tree, a strand of barbed wire was wrapped around it from ground level beyond the height that

ABANDONED BEAVER COLONY

This meadow was formerly a series of beaver ponds. Remnants of several beaver dams can still be seen. Active colonies of beaver kept these dams in repair impounding the water which flooded the meadow.

After removing most of the aspen and willow for food and dams the beaver moved out. The ponds have silted in and the dam severed so now the stream is cutting into the old pond bottom lowering the water table and permitting invasion of pine trees.

Active colonies may be seen one mile upstream on right. ➡

Sign overlooking an abandoned beaver colony in Rocky Mountain National Park.

a beaver could reach. A beaver started to cut it, but every time it pricked its nose on one of the barbs it moved up or down and cut as deeply as it could. The beaver never felled the tree, but it did cut a deep spiral groove in it from ground level to as high as it could reach. Later the tree was cut down, and the length of log was put on display in the museum.

In another instance where beavers seemed to demonstrate a wry satisfaction in thwarting man, they had built a large dam immediately upstream from a bridge across a farm lane. The landowner was concerned about its road being flooded, so he regularly made a break in the dam to lower the water level, and the following night, the beavers repaired the damage. This went on for some time until the beavers completely plugged the space under the bridge with material that was most difficult to dislodge. That done, they added insult to injury by abandoning the pond. They moved half a mile upstream and started a new one.

Beavers have repeatedly demonstrated that they can learn from experience, especially if that experience has been of an unpleasant

The new dam and small pond built immediately behind the sign indicating all the reasons why the beavers abandoned the area. There are times when the beaver almost seems to display a sardonic sense of humor.

nature. Such an encounter often results in a scent shunning, trap-wise, extremely wary individual.

Every state now has a department that is in charge of wildlife management within its borders. These are known by different titles, but their duties are similar. A number of them have employees who are expert outdoorsmen of long experience and wise in the ways of wildlife.

Today there is an increasing number of instances where the presence of wildlife comes into conflict with human activities. As beavers have been extending their range, there are now growing numbers of complaints about beaver damage. In such instances the only solution is to remove them. In many instances, these expert trappers are called in to capture and relocate the problem animals.

After a frustrating experience, one of these men is reputed to have said, "Given time I can take the most wily fox that I ever knew, but a trap-wise beaver can not only beat me at every trick I have ever learned, but when he has done it, he is too stupid to know that there has ever been a contest."

49

2

The Beaver Fur Trade

Nothing about the beaver's appearance, habits, or way of life give the slightest hint of its impact on the course of history or the degree to which it was responsible for the exploration, settlement, and development of a continent. The beaver is a peaceful creature and desires only to be left alone to pursue its normal manner of living. Yet, he was the unwitting and unwilling cause of over two centuries of prolonged competition, intrigue, and conflict that involved individuals, organizations, colonists, Native Americans, and foreign governments. It was a time of intermittent confrontation ranging from sporadic minor skirmishes to periods of prolonged costly and bloody wars. At one time or another these conflicts involved Holland, Sweden, Spain, and Portugal as well as native tribes and colonists. The most prolonged and hardest fought wars were between France and England. These conflicts did not come to an end until two wars had been fought between the American colonies and the Mother Country.

It is because of the beaver that the chief language north of the Mexican border is English, except for Quebec, rather than French, Spanish, Dutch, Swedish, or Portuguese and that most of the laws and customs are patterned after those of England rather than France, Spain, Holland, Sweden, or Portugal.

All of this came about as a result of the superior quality of the beaver's fur for although there were other animals whose skins brought higher prices in the fur auctions of Europe, those of the beaver had the widest market. The greatest demand for beaver skins was for the making of hats, largely because the soft underfur matted down to make felt of superior quality.

Beaver fur could be made into hats of a great variety of shapes and colors which held their shape and wore well. The hats of the Pilgrim Fathers were made from beaver fur, as were the broad-brimmed hats of William Penn, the plumed hats of the Cavaliers, and the ornate hats of "the ladies of fashion."

The demand for beaver fur was so great that in their quest for its pelt, trappers sought out the beaver in the most remote areas. Traders

51

followed trappers into the wilderness to bargain for their catches of beaver skins and other furs. Westwardbound settlers followed the routes discovered by the mountain men and traders, and tradesmen, artisans, speculators, builders, and bankers soon followed the settlers. Because of the beaver, the exploration and settlement of North America was hastened by at least half a century. The animal was the major cause of the tide of westward migration and settlement from the eastern states that rolled relentlessly across the country to the Oregon Territory and California. Thus, all the land that lies between the Mexican and Canadian borders constitutes the major part of the country known as the United States of America. Had it not been for the beaver, the makeup of the present-day map of North America might have a much different appearance.

In addition to the heavy demand for beaver fur, dried castor glands became an important item of trade. For countless generations, Indians used them in making medicines, but in Europe they were put to another use. Beaver musk became an important ingredient in the making of perfume. Those were the days before modern plumbing, and the taking of baths was neither convenient nor generally popular. In fact, there were those that believed that it was downright unhealthy. As a consequence, whenever there were social gatherings or meetings for other purposes, there was a heavy demand for incense and perfumes to override and mask body odors.

Establishment of Trade Routes in the Old World

The beaver was propelled willy-nilly into its role as a maker of history and a builder of empires by a series of events that occurred many centuries before and thousands of miles distant. When King Solomon built the Temple in Jerusalem, he did it with the help and materials obtained from his friend, Hiram, King of Tyre. When completed, it was probably the most magnificent edifice of worship that the world had ever seen with its rare woods, fine linens, gold, silver, and precious stones. The treasure it contained, by today's values, would be worth several billions of United States dollars.

These were prosperous years for the two kingdoms, and a large part of their wealth was based upon trade. Caravans to and from the Far East crossed and recrossed them. The western end of the journey was either the port city of Tyre or Sidon. There the merchandise was unloaded and stowed aboard merchant ships of Phoenician traders and transported thence to harbor cities in Europe and North Africa. From the East were brought silks, spices, and precious stones, and on the return journeys they carried wool, amber from the Baltic, frankincense, myrrh, pearls from the Persian Gulf, and the famous purple dye made from snails from Tyre. At a later date, when the

Roman Empire was at the height of its power, there was a very active demand for this dye, but the estimated cost of the toga of the Roman nobleman who "wore the purple" would amount to over five thousand present-day United States dollars.

The route followed some of the world's most rugged and inhospitable terrain, and every mile traveled held the possibility of grave danger, not only from the elements but also from attacks by bandits on land and pirates by sea. Therefore, every caravan followed a well-travelled route with regular stations where there were opportunities to rest and obtain supplies. Every caravan was composed of a large number of pack animals and men, including impressive numbers of armed guards. On the sea, every merchant ship had to be prepared to repel attacks by pirates. That trade expanded and continued at an accelerated pace during the hundreds of years that the Roman Empire dominated Europe, Britain, North Africa, and a large part of Asia. It continued during the Middle Ages and flourished during the Renaissance.

In 1453, the Turks captured Constantinople and gained control of the western end of the trade route across Asia Minor. As a consequence, the best minds of Europe sought ways to circumvent the Turks by finding a new route to the Indies. Christopher Columbus, an Italian navigator who believed that the earth was round concluded that the best route to the Indies was to sail west. He convinced Queen Isabella of Spain that his plan was feasible, and she furnished him with three small ships with supplies and crews, the Nina, Pinta, and Santa Maria. The navigator left Spain for a long and perilous journey into the unknown.

The New World: Discovery and Exploitation

On October 12, 1492, Columbus landed on an island in the Caribbean, which he named San Salvador. Exploring farther, he touched on the island of Cuba, which he first took to be the island of Japan, and from there to Haiti, which again he hopefully identified as Japan. So certain was he that he had arrived at the Indies, that he referred to the people living there as "Indians," an egregious misnomer that still persists. Even after three more voyages in 1493, 1498, and 1502–1504, when he died in 1506, he still believed that he had reached the Orient.

There were two problems that Columbus did not know existed when he set sail west to reach the Far East. The first was that two large continents connected by an isthmus lay athwart his passage, and the second was that beyond those great land masses lay a much larger ocean than the one he was about to cross. Moreover, from none of his trips did Columbus return with the holds of his ships laden with cargoes of high value.

In the meantime, Vasco de Gama found a route to India by sailing down the west coast of Africa, around the Cape of Good Hope, and up the east coast. He arrived in Calcutta in 1498 and returned to Lisbon in 1499 with a cargo of spices and jewels. Lisbon thus became the depot for oriental trade. Queen Isabella believed that the greatest accomplishment during her lifetime was the expulsion of the Moors in 1492, not the discovery of two new continents.

Instead of being named Columbia after its discoverer, the new land took its name after a Florentine businessman and voyager, Amerigo Vespucci, sometimes also known as Americus Vespucies. He penned a number of widely circulated letters in which he claimed credit for the discovery of the mainland before Columbus. In 1507, the year after the death of Columbus, a German geographer proposed that the new world be named America.

For a number of years, Spain regarded the Atlantic Ocean as a private lake, and in 1493, Pope Alexander VI granted to Spain all the lands that Columbus had discovered. This ran counter to a claim by Portugal, which until then had been upheld by the Pope. He settled the dispute by drawing a line of demarcation which ran from north to south some 370 degrees west of the Cape Verde Islands. Any lands lying east of that line belonged to Portugal by right of discovery, and those west of that line to Spain. The coastline of Brazil was on the east side of the line and was settled by Portugal, and the rest of South America, Central America, and the southern portion of North America, including California, were first settled by Spain, thus accounting for the fact that in all of South America today, Brazil is the only country where Portuguese is the official language rather than Spanish.

Out of the base at Santo Domingo, or Hispañola, Spain's explorer captains led expeditions to Cuba, Central America, and Florida in search of gold, silver, and precious stones that existed in fabulous quantities in the fabled city of El Dorado. They were always seeking the elusive new route to the Indies. One of these explorers, who was no longer young, Ponce de Leon, also searched in vain for the Fountain of Youth in Florida. At a later date, Coronado set forth on his vain search for the seven golden cities of Cibola. In only two instances were the Spaniards successful: in 1521, when Cortez overcame and plundered the Aztecs and a decade later when Pizarro and a small band of Spanish soldiers overthrew and looted the Incas in Peru. Long before other European nations established permanent colonies in the New World, Spain had established such settlements in the New World and had established a vast empire in both North and South America.

The decline of the Spanish Empire began in 1556 when Phillip II became emperor. He became involved in a number of anti-Protestant crusades against the Netherlands and England which drained Spain's supply of gold and silver to pay for her armies and for supplies for her colonies. Much of the money went into the hands of Flemish and German bankers, and on the high seas, Drake, Hawkins, and Frobisher "singed the beard of the King of Spain" by their captures of Spanish galleons laden with treasure. Spain had also expelled the Jews and the Moors and thus lacked the merchants and the craftsmen who could have enriched her by commerce. The heaviest blow fell in 1588 when the giant armada of Spanish and Portuguese men-of-war sent against England was scattered and destroyed by Drake's ships. A violent storm drove aground many others that had managed to escape.

Spain never became directly involved in the fur trade, but the gold, silver, and emeralds that her ships brought back from Mexico and South America did play a major role. Considerable sums of it found its way into the hands of those who would later use them as the means of exchange in the buying, processing, and selling of the furs brought out from North America. The Spaniards also made another contribution by bringing the horse and the burro and crossing them to produce the mule. They developed highly effective ways to use the horse, the burro, and especially the mule to carry packs and to transport heavy loads long distances over rough country. This form of transportation was widely used by the beaver trappers of the nineteenth century.

In addition to Spain, England, Holland, and France, Portugal sent out expeditions to find a safe route to the Far East by sailing west. Also there was always the hope of finding treasure as the Spaniards had done in Mexico and Peru. Neither goal was ever achieved on any of these voyages, but in every instance the captain returned with interesting stories concerning the places that they had visited. Even though there was little or nothing of commercial value brought back to recompense those who had financed the expeditions, in future years those discoveries resulted in permanent settlements that were highly profitable.

The voyage that eventually resulted in the development of the fur trade was made in 1497 by an Italian, John Cabot (Giovanni Caboto). He sailed with the financial backing of the Merchants of Bristol during the reign of England's Henry VII. He explored the east coast of North America from Newfoundland to Hatteras and discovered the Grand Banks where fish were so abundant that they could be brought up with baskets. The English were not duly impressed that he had discovered an area where codfish and other species abounded because Protestant England was far more interested in beef and mutton than fish as sources of food. Things were quite different in Catholic Europe. In a long letter dated December 1497, the ambassador from Milan wrote to the Duke of Milan as follows. "They affirm that the sea is full of fish, which are not only taken with a net, but also with a basket, a stone being fastened to it in order to keep it in the water. . . . They took so many fish that this kingdom will no longer have need of Iceland" (16).

If England was reluctant to take advantage of Cabot's discovery of the Grand Banks, France definitely was not. Soon after the news was received in Europe, France sent out ships with crews to fish for cod and the other species to be found there in such abundance. Portugal soon followed France's example.

In 1527, Bristol's John Rut, who was seeking the Strait of Anian, put in at St. John's Harbor in Newfoundland and saw eleven sails of Normans and Bretons. In 1539, a shipbuilder of Bristol made a revolutionary discovery. He demonstrated the principle of sailing into the wind. This made it possible to make faster time in crossing and recrossing the Atlantic. By 1603, there were six hundred ships on the banks. Between the time of Cabot's discovery and that date, the Basques were operating a whaling station where the whales their ships brought in were processed. The Basques began hunting whales off the east coast early in the sixteenth century.

At that time there was no way to get fresh fish from the Grand Banks to Europe. Therefore, they were salted and dried before they were transported. To accomplish this, it was necessary to build drying racks of wood, very much like those one sees along the east coast of Canada today. When the fishing fleets had returned home at the end of the season, those empty racks were an inviting source of ready-cut, dry firewood. To preserve this convenient resource, the fishermen gave gifts to the Indians to be certain that they would not be destroyed.

Most of the tools used by the Indians were made of stone except for a very few items made of native copper, and because of its superior cutting efficiency, one of the most highly prized gifts was the steel knife. In their contacts with the Europeans, the Indians also saw them using axes, saws, adzes, and nails made of iron or steel. Europeans caught fish on sharp steel hooks attached to strong lines made of linen, and they cooked in kettles made of brass or copper. They mended clothes with steel needles and thread, and they wore garments made of cloth rather than skins of animals. The Indians came to prefer cloth over buckskin, and as a result they began to exchange furs for some of these items.

The Beginnings of the Beaver Fur Trade
The French

The fur trade began more by accident than by intent, but once started, it grew at a rapid rate. Those most responsible were the

56

Normans. Years before the first trading posts were established, they traveled inland and traded with the Indians, lived with them, hunted with them, and had half-Indian families. In so doing, they learned the language and customs of the woodland Indians and earned their trust and friendship. To the woodland Indians, the beaver was as important as the buffalo became to the tribes of the open prairies. As a food, beaver meat was held in highest esteem, and roast beaver tail was deemed a special delicacy. Beaver teeth were used to make cutting

Side view of the head of a beaver showing the incisor teeth.

tools, and piles of beaver skins served as bedding and sometimes as covers. However, more often they slept under blankets made from inch wide sections of skins of the Snowshoe Hare twisted into ropes and woven into blankets. The Swampy Crees of northern Canada still use

57

them, and they make an exceptionally warm blanket if one does not object to being covered with rabbit hairs upon rising in the morning.

Swampy Cree with snowshoe hair blankets which he was offering to sell to the author as he took the picture.

When the glaciers moved down from the north, for centuries the land was covered with a thick blanket of ice that was well over a mile deep in many places. As they pushed their way south, they gouged out, pushed ahead, picked up, and carried away vast amounts of rock and earth. When they retreated, they left behind thousands of depressions that filled with water, among them the Great Lakes that extend to the center of the continent, and thousands of smaller lakes, ponds, and kettle holes. When the weather became warmer and the ice retreated, trees moved in and covered the area. This became prime beaver country.

When the first bands of wandering hunters crossed over on the land bridge to North America, they found a land studded with ponds and lakes and laced with water courses ranging in size from small streams to mighty rivers. Ample archaeological evidence confirms the fact that these Native Americans traveled and traded extensively. For winter travel and transportation they invented snowshoes and the toboggan. For travel when the ice was out, they developed a highly efficient mode of water transportation, the birch-bark canoe. This was an entirely different craft from the one dug out of a log and was so light that a man could carry one across land from one body of water to another. The Europeans were impressed with the craft to the degree that they sometimes took them home to show to potential financial backers.

The Norman traders learned to take full advantage of the canoe to carry trade goods inland and to bring out furs to harbors where they were stowed in the holds of ships bound for Dieppe or Rouen. In the meantime, Bretons were sending them to San Malo. From the Norman fur traders there developed a special breed of men, the *coureurs-de-bois* and the *voyageurs.* They took full advantage of the capabilities of the canoe and developed the large freighter canoe that could carry heavy loads, required several paddlers, and was seaworthy to the extent that it could travel on the Great Lakes in times of storm. To a land barrier that had to be crossed to get from one body of water to another they gave a name that is part of our vocabulary today, *portage.* The distance could vary from a few hundred feet to several miles: as an example, the one around Niagara Falls to get from Lake Ontario to Lake Erie. The same word, *portage,* is used to describe the crossing with canoes and equipment. In their trips across portages, it was sometimes necessary to transport items that were of odd shapes and often very heavy. To carry those loads they devised the tumpline. This is a long piece of leather with a wide spot in the middle, long enough to go across the forehead. From there it rapidly tapers down to a width of approximately an inch on either side. The ends are tied around the object that is to be transported. For smaller objects they used the pack basket that was developed by the eastern woodland Indians. Tumplines and pack baskets are still used by trappers, hunters, and guides in eastern Canada. There are reports that pianos have been taken to inland trading posts by canoe and across portages.

The *coureurs-de-bois* and the *voyageurs* were able to live off the land like the Indians; in fact, many were part Indian. Expeditions to explore the interior of the continent sent out by Spain usually required a well-armed party of soldiers as an escort. In contrast, those of France were carried out by adventurous individuals and small groups that returned from their journeys not only with information, but often with loads of

furs of great value as well. Unlike the Spanish in their futile search for
El Dorado, the French explorers found a source of renewable wealth in
the form of beaver skins, and those that had been slept on over a period
of several months and had become matted down and saturated with
human body oil made the best felt. These were known as *castor gras
d'hiver,* or fat beaver. From the Indian's point of view, it was an
excellent arrangement. They could sleep on a pile of beaver skins all
winter and sell them to a trader in the spring.

The beaver trade started along the lower St. Lawrence River.
Unfortunately, the demand for beaver pelts outstripped the ability of
beavers to replenish their numbers, and it was necessary to travel
farther and farther inland to find places where they were still abundant.
Traders traveled up the St. Lawrence and followed the Ottawa and
Dumoine Rivers to their headwaters. There, in an area where there are
thousands of lakes and ponds, they found prime beaver country. When
the supply of pelts became scarce there, they traveled the full length of
the Great Lakes and followed their tributaries inland. Eventually their
exploring parties traveled down the Mississippi to New Orleans. Not
all these explorers were traders, *coureurs-de-bois,* and *voyageurs.* Many
like Père Marquette were missionaries.

Originally Spain had claimed sovereignty over all the lands,
except for Brazil, in North America, South America, and those in
between. In defiance of Spanish claims, in 1539, Francis I, King of
France, sent Jacques Cartier to the new lands, and he sailed up the St.
Lawrence River to the present location of Montreal. His attempt to start
a settlement with a few criminals failed miserably. When the fur trade
began to flourish, it was evident that measures required to protect
it, and among these measures was the decision to establish French
settlements along the coast. Forty criminals were marooned on Sable
Island in 1598, but only eleven were still there five years later. Another
colonizer, Pierre Chauvin, built the first trading post in North America
at Tadoussac in 1600. He had agreed to transport fifty settlers but
managed to transport only sixteen street beggars and criminals, all of
whom made off at once and lived with the Indians. Chauvin did not
trade long at Tadoussac as he lost his monopoly because of his failure
to colonize.

Colonization began to be discussed seriously in the court of King
Henry of Navarre, especially after it was learned that English and
Dutch ships were prowling these northern waters. There was news that
an English seaman, Gosnold, had visited the south of the St. Lawrence
in 1602. He traded with the natives and sailed home with a cargo of
furs, sassafras, and other oddities.

A company was established, and De Chastes was named
president. In 1603, Champlain and Pontgravé sailed out to find the best

sites for a colony and trading posts. Champlain occupied himself with exploring, and Pontgravé engaged in a brisk barter of pelts. They returned home with enough furs to pay for the trip and to show a small profit. It was the understanding that New France would stand or fall according to the success of the fur trade. After De Chastes' death, De Monts was made the new president. To avoid repeating the mistakes of his predecessors, De Monts offered inducements for respectable people to emigrate and in 1604 set out with about one hundred thirty colonists. They settled first on St. Croix Island, and after a disastrous winter during which many died of scurvy, they moved to the mainland and settled Port Royal. In the spring of 1607, Pontgravé brought to the colony the bad news that the monopoly had been withdrawn. On August 11, the colonists sailed for France.

Champlain founded Quebec in 1608, and in 1610, Port Royal was reestablished. That was the year that King Henry was assassinated, and the queen, Marie de Medici, was regent. What had been bad times for the Huguenots were about to become worse.

The Huguenots were Protestant and a solid middle class composed of artisans, tradesmen, and professionals. They could have established highly successful communities in America. Instead, these "Heretics" were subjected to years of discrimination, persecution and death. During the reign of Catherine de Medici, on the night of St. Bartholomeu, August 23–24, 1572, several thousands of Huguenots were massacred in Paris.

At the death of Henry III, Henry IV ascended the throne, and he made every effort to heal religious differences. He promulgated the Edict of Nantes, which proclaimed religious freedom, and during his lifetime the Huguenots were free from persecution. With his death their rights were gradually stripped away, were withdrawn completely during the reign of Louis XIV, and were abolished completely in 1685 with the revocation of the Edict of Nantes. This led to the immigration of 400,000 Huguenots to Prussia, Holland, Switzerland, the British Isles, and by clandestine methods, by way of Holland and England to America, not to New France but to the English colonies, mostly in New York and New England. One of these communities is New Paltz, New York. In the old part of town there are several fine buildings that were built and occupied by the Huguenots who settled there.

Canada was colonized, and the new commerce of the fur trade was initiated because of the foresight and steadfastness of four men, De Monts, Champlain, Pontgravé, and Poutrincourt. By the time the first census was made in 1666–1667, there were 3215 souls plus 1200 men of the King's troops. Things however had not gone smoothly. In 1613, Port Royal was destroyed by Argyle of Jamestown. In 1628, eighteen vessels left Dieppe with settlers and supplies. A fleet of English privateers was waiting for them in the Gulf of St. Lawrence, captured

61

them, and took them back to England as prizes of war. At the time, England and France were at war.

Through the fur trade, France had explored and claimed an empire that covered a large part of the North American continent, but she had already committed the first three gross errors in judgment that would cause her to lose it. The first was her refusal to permit the Huguenots to become settlers in New France. Instead, they attempted to start settlements with criminals with disastrous results. It was not easy for a number of years to induce respectable French citizens to leave their homes to establish settlements in the wilderness.

The second error was committed by Champlain. In 1609, with a band of twenty Frenchmen, he joined a war party of sixty Algonquin Indians on an expedition against the Iroquois. The Indians traveled in twenty-four canoes. The French had their supplies in a shallop, which would not pass the falls at Chambly. Champlain made the difficult decision to send the shallop back with most of its crew. With two French companions, he accompanied the Indians on into Iroquois territory.

They came upon the Iroquois at Ticonderoga. The muskets of the French killed a number of Iroquois and when they saw their chiefs fall dead, the rest fled in terror. The French won an easy victory with their guns but in doing so they incurred the undying hatred of the Iroquois. This hatred would be later exploited and used with devastating effect by the English against the French.

Two years before Champlain and his Algonquin allies routed the Iroquois at Ticonderoga, another event occurred that challenged the French control of the fur trade. On May 13, 1607, Captain John Smith arrived at Jamestown with one hundred five Cavaliers in three ships and founded the first permanent English colony in the New World. In 1624, the Dutch left eight men from the ship *New Netherland* on Manhattan Island. The rest sailed for Albany, which the Dutch named Fort Orange. In 1626, Peter Minuet bought Manhattan Island from the Indians.

In 1620, a little ship named *The Mayflower* left Plymouth, England with one hundred three religious dissidents. The Puritans, as they were known, were supposed to land in Virginia, but because of bad weather and poor navigation, they landed in the vicinity of Plymouth Rock on the shores of present-day Massachusetts instead. After a disastrous winter during which half of them died, they founded the Plymouth Colony, which grew rapidly in size and importance.

Within less than a decade, England and Holland had established three permanent colonies on the east coast of North America. These grew rapidly and others soon followed. With these colonies as bases, both Holland and England became heavily involved in the fur trade,

Bull Elk in
Yellowstone Park

Great Blue Heron

Rocky Mountain Big Horn Sheep

Redhead Drake

Beaver Ponds, Banff, Canada

Western Beaver Pond
with canal in foreground

Rocky Mountain Goat

Wood Ducks

Moose cow and calf
in the Canadian
Rockies

and as their traders moved north, they often came into armed conflict with the French.

France paid a heavy price for the help that Champlain gave the Hurons against the Iroquois in 1609. The Iroquois had a powerful confederation, a long memory, and an abiding hatred of the French and their Indian allies. In 1649, they sent out an expedition against the Hurons with devastating effect. Very few managed to escape; most were killed or taken captive. Among the weapons that they used against the Hurons were firearms that they had obtained from the Dutch and learned to use with deadly effect.

Because of the Iroquois animosity against the French, all of North America south of Lake Ontario and Lake Erie was hostile territory. French traders were not welcome, although those from Holland and England were.

The third error in judgment, which contributed to France's losing not only the revenue from the fur trade but her empire in North America as well, was committed by the Governor of Three Rivers. It is ironic that three Frenchmen unwittingly made impact on a course of events that would make history, and within a century, contribute heavily to the loss of an empire for France. The first was Pierre Esprit Radisson, one of the most flamboyant and colorful characters associated with the fur trade. No single individual had a greater impact on its future. He was brought to Three Rivers as a boy. He was captured by the Mohawks and escaped approximately two years later. In 1652, he settled in Three Rivers.

The second was Radisson's brother-in-law, Medard Chouart Sieur des Groseilliers, and the third was the Governor of Three Rivers, who earned his dubious place in history as the bumbling bureaucrat who made one of the costliest blunders in the history of North America.

In 1658, Radisson and Groseilliers set out for present-day Lake Nipissing, then known as Lac des Castors, or in English, Lake of the Beavers. They made an overland journey that took them to the shores of the great bay that Henry Hudson had discovered. The country was claimed by England but had been almost completely neglected since the discovery. They explored the Lake Superior region and the headwaters of the Mississippi, and they were the first white men to come in contact with the Crees and the Sioux or Dakotas of the Great Plains. They returned to Three Rivers in 1663 with sixty canoes loaded to the gunnels with beaver skins and other furs. Radisson also devised a plan that would open a vast new trading territory, that of building trading posts at the mouths of the rivers that flow into the waters of Hudson Bay. The advantages to this plan were obvious. The Hudson Bay drainage system provided a vast, new potential area where trading could be conducted directly with the Indians in their own territory. Supplies and trade goods could be brought in by ship and on the return journey a cargo of beaver pelts and other furs could be stowed aboard for shipment directly to France. This would cut down on the difficult and expensive transport of furs by canoe and portage. Not the least of these advantages was the removal of the threat by the Iroquois. Their prowling war parties lurked along the rivers, and at every opportunity, they ambushed and plundered expeditions headed downriver on their way to market their furs. When the Iroquois returned home with their loot, they found Dutch traders eager to bargain for them.

Whether prompted by crass cupidity, gross stupidity, or the act of a bumbling bureaucrat of the "I-am-only-carrying-out-my-orders" type, or a combination thereof, the Governor of Three Rivers made a decision to turn a deaf ear to Radisson's plan. In addition, on the pretext that they had not paid for the proper license before starting on their expedition and with a specious accusation of insubordination, he confiscated their furs.

It is difficult to determine the value of those furs in the present-day market; however, it is safe to say that the sales value at a present-day auction would be many hundreds of thousands of dollars and in the buying power of those days, this represented a princely fortune. Radisson and Groseilliers spent three years trying to get proper recompense for their loss and backing for their plan but were successful in neither.

After surviving wrecking storms at sea and the Dutch naval guns, Redisson and Groseilliers arrived in England. A chance meeting with Sir George Carteret, Vice Chamberlain of the Household of Charles II and one of the original Proprietors of Carolina, brought them in contact with a group of powerful merchants and the King himself.

The British

English merchants had suffered severely from the war with Holland. London was a blackened wasteland. The great fire had consumed 13,000 houses, 90 churches, the guild halls, and counting houses. The plague had struck London, and over 68,000 lives were lost out of a population of 400,000. In addition to their losses to the Dutch by sea, many had lost friends, members of their families, employees, and business associates to the plague and their homes and places of business to the fire. There was trouble overseas also. The Iroquois had signed a treaty of friendship with the French. The year 1666 was not a good one, and Radisson and Groseilliers as well as the merchants were ready to learn about any plan whereby they might recoup past losses combined with the prospect of handsome future profit. When Sir George Carteret introduced Radisson and Groseilliers to various merchants, they found eager listeners to the plan which the Governor of Three Rivers had rejected. Their audience had a bit of difficulty with names, however. English ears could deal with "Mr. Radisson, or Radizon," without much difficulty, but Medard Chouart Sieur des Groseilliers, was not as easy. In London, he became "Mr. Gooseberry," which of course is the direct translation of the French into English.

Sir George Carteret introduced Radisson and Groseilliers not only to men of influence but also to King Charles II himself, who became an eager listener to the point where he did an unheard-of thing. He actually paid them forty shillings a week to regale him with tales of their wilderness adventures. The plan had hearty approval and the blessing of the King, but scraping together sufficient funds to implement it was another matter. It was 1668 before this came to pass.

The funds were eventually provided by Prince Rupert; the Duke of Albermarle; the Earls of Arlington, Shaftesbury and Craven; John Portman, the goldsmith; and various other interested persons. Two small ships were outfitted, *The Eaglet* and *The Nonesuch*. Prince Rupert inspected them, drank toasts to the success of the venture, and they sailed from Gravesend. Radisson was on *The Eaglet*, Groseilliers on *The Nonesuch*. In spite of Radisson's objections, the Captain of *The Eaglet* refused to enter Hudson Strait, turned about and returned home. Fortunately, the captain of *The Nonesuch* was a hardier mariner. The ship spent the winter in the bay, and it was a very depressing time for the crew. The weather was most severe, but Groseilliers employed the time in active trading with the Indians. In the spring, *The Nonesuch* sailed home loaded with furs. Not only did they pay the costs of the expedition, but they yielded a profit as well. Those who had financed the expedition were delighted, and plans were rapidly made to develop trade in the Hudson Bay region. For France this was a fateful decision for she was destined to pay a very heavy price for the sixty canoe loads of furs that her agent had confiscated.

On May 2, 1670, Charles II, King of England, granted a Royal Charter to "Governor and Company of Adventurers of England Trading into Hudson's Bay." The designated Governor was the King's cousin, Prince Rupert, and the territory was to be known as Rupert's Land. The Royal Charter was written on five sheets of parchment and is preserved in the Board Room of Hudson's Bay House in Bishopgate, London.

The cost to the King was only his signature. He granted

> ... unto them and their successors sole Trade and Commerce of all those Seas, Streights, Bays, Rivers, Creeks and Soundes, in whatever Latitude they shal bee, that lye within the Streights commonly called Hudson's Streights, together with all the Landes,

Countryes and Territories upon the Coasts and Confynes . . . which are now actually possessed by any of our Subjects or any other Christian Prince.

That Royal Charter, couched in the flowery language of the seventeenth century and spread across twenty-seven square feet of parchment, by today's standards is unnecessarily long and needlessly ornate, but it is explicit down to the most minute detail. It conveyed to Prince Rupert, his associates, and their successors the sole right to occupy and exercise absolute domination over the vast territory designated as Rupert's Land. The provision, "whether claimed by England or by subjects of any other Christian Prince or State," could only have referred to France. Power was given to make laws, judge all civil and criminal laws according to the laws of England, make treaties, settle disputes, punish offenses, erect forts, employ armed forces, and call upon the armed forces of England. In brief, this amounted to total jurisdiction over everything in the water, on the land, or under the earth in Rupert's Land, namely the entire Hudson's Bay drainage system. This is the area of Canada west of the Alleghenies, east of the Rockies, and on the south, within forty-seven miles of the Great Lakes. The area of Hudson Bay alone is 281,908 square miles. For comparison, the area of Texas is 267,338 square miles. In addition, the Hudson's Bay Company was and is the only private company that can fly its emblem on a nation's flag. It appeared on the red ensign flag where it was flown above Hudson's Bay post or from a Hudson's Bay ship.

On the coat of arms of Hudson's Bay Company is "one elk, rampant and four beavers sable." The "elk" is not the Wapiti but the American Moose. Beneath is the motto, "Pro Pelle Cutem," literally, a skin for a skin. As was the custom in granting a monopoly, there was a provision that the company "seek out a route to the South Sea" and a further provision that whenever Charles or future heirs to the throne visited Rupert's Land, they were to receive "two beavers sable as a sign of fealty." This was done on the two-hundred-fiftieth anniversary of the founding of Hudson's Bay company in 1920 when the Prince of Wales visited Canada.

Hudson's Bay Company has had a remarkable record in conducting its operations. From the beginning, its greatest strength has been its success in attracting, selecting, and holding men of integrity and capability to manage its outposts. Hudson's Bay Company was organized and has been largely owned by Englishmen, but the Factors who managed the enterprises in Canada have been predominantly Scots. They frequently married Indian wives, and today, many of the Swampy Crees have Scottish names and speak English with a rich Scottish burr.

The policy of Hudson's Bay Company can best be described as enlightened self-interest. The most convincing evidence that it was based upon sound judgment is the fact that the Company has been trading for fur with the Swampy Cree Indians of the Hudson Bay drainage system for well over three centuries. The posts were

Silas Wesley, a Swampy Cree Indian, with Canada Geese. He support his family as an expert hunting, trapping and fishing guide. He was the "chief actor" in the documentary film *Land of the Blue Goose* by Earl L. Hilfiker.

designated sometimes as forts, sometimes as Factories. Hudson's Bay Company had the authority but never incurred the expense of building and providing garrisons for forts. Moose Factory, built on an island in the Moose River at the headwaters of James Bay, is one of the oldest and largest of all the Hudson's Bay Company trading posts. The buildings are made of wood, painted white. In front of the trading post are a small cannon and the press used to compact bales of pelts before

Hudson's Bay Trading Post Moose Factory. This post is located on Moose Island at the mouth of the Moose River. Picture was taken at low tide. Note the H. B. C. plane in the foreground.

they were loaded in the holds of ships bound for England. The agent that the company appointed to manage the post was known as the Factor. He was given full powers of discretion to manage the post, or Factory, and its district as long as it turned a profit. In emergencies he could call upon the armed forces of Britain to defend it.

To the Indians, the Factor was the most important man in the district. Before leaving for the trapping season, he advanced to the Indian families the food and supplies necessary to last until the spring when the trappers returned with their loads of furs. The Indians knew the cost of each item, and the goods were and are of high quality. Hudson's Bay blankets remain highly prized possessions today. A four-point blanket represents the cost of four large beaver skins, a three-and-a-half point blanket, the cost of three large beaver skins and one small one. The Hudson's Bay axe was especially designed as a trade item. It has a full-length handle and a full-width cutting edge, but it is narrower across the eye where the handle is inserted to cut down on the weight and make it easier to carry than a regular woodsman's axe.

The pelt baling press and old cannon at Moose Island. This press was used to compact the bales of pelts before they were loaded in the holds of ships bound for England. The author is at the left and his friend, Robert Montgomery, is at the right.

From the beginning, Hudson's Bay Company has lived up to its motto, "Pro Pelle Cutem," roughly meaning value for value. It has depended upon the Indians to bring out the furs, and in turn, it has looked after their interests. Many have lived out their lives as pensioners of the Company when they were no longer able to follow their trap lines. Employees of the Company are regularly sent out for medical and dental treatment. From the beginning, it was strictly against Company policy to use whiskey in its trade with the Indians. Two items of trade that were introduced at an early date were tea and oatmeal. They also brought cloth, needles, thread, and glass beads. Today the Crees that live in the vicinity of Hudson Bay live largely in a moose, goose, and beaver economy. From the moose they get meat and leather; from the geese, they get meat and goose down; and from the beaver, they acquire food and skins that they can sell to pay for the other items they need or desire. They are still trading with the Hudson's Bay Company in very much the same way as their forefathers.

Family of Silas Wesley preparing geese to be smoked as part of their winter food supply. Goose down is an item for which there is a wide market. The family, including his grandmother, sister, wife, daughter, and a small baby, will spend the winter in the 9×12 tent behind them.

Over the years the Swampy Crees have developed a special craft for which they are noted. Moosehide is often cured by smoking, but the Crees have developed a special process of tanning whereby the leather is bleached and turns white. For many years glass beads have been used to decorate the leather work, but more often it is decorated with silk embroidery, which they have developed into a high form of art. Visitors to the Anglican Church on Moose Factory Island have marveled at the exquisite beauty of the altar cloths made of silk-embroidered bleached moosehide.

The Hudson's Bay Company's control over the beaver trade has not gone unchallenged. The French captured and held most of the forts from 1686 to 1714. Later it came into conflict with the Northwestern Company, which had its headquarters in Montreal, and Fort Williams at the head of Lake Superior. Before the two companies merged in 1821, there was armed conflict and bloodshed. In 1840, native peoples challenged the company dominance. After the Confederation was established in 1867, Canada bought approximately seven million acres of fertile land, which now forms several of its provinces, for 300,000

British pounds sterling from Hudson's Bay Company. Today Hudson's Bay Company is largely a trading enterprise, and there are free traders operating in competition in the areas where Hudson's Bay Company once enjoyed full trading rights.

The founding of Hudson's Bay Company was one of three events that occurred in the year 1670 that led to Britain's full-scale entry into the fur trade and eventually into armed conflict with the French. The second was the news that a new town had sprung up along the coast of the Carolinas. Named after the King, Charles Town had an excellent harbor, which opened to the English a lucrative new fur-trading area along the Ohio and Mississippi Rivers that had been closed to French traders by the Iroquois and their allies. New France was now being squeezed by English forces from both north and south. Hudson's Bay Company was extending its range south, and traders and settlers from English coastal colonies were rapidly moving northward.

The third event was the death of Admiral Penn, who during his life had generously "loaned" to the King sums of money that totalled over sixteen thousand pounds. These monies had largely been used to support the King's gambling habits. William Penn, the admiral's son, became a Quaker, a sect that was persecuted, and many members were in prison. The Duke of York protected William and brought him to the attention of the King. In 1681, Charles II issued another Royal Charter, this one to Admiral Penn's son, William, giving him title to a huge tract of land in the New World to be known as Pennsylvania, or Penn's Woods, named after the old admiral. At the cost of a few strokes of his pen, Charles II paid a debt and also ridded England of a group of unwanted dissidents.

The territory granted by Royal Charter to William Penn and his followers had originally been settled by Swedes and claimed by Sweden along with Delaware and New Jersey. The Dutch took the land away from Sweden and in turn had it taken from them by England in 1664, the year that it also claimed New York.

William Penn settled Pennsylvania with Quaker refugees and any others who wished to settle there to be free from religious persecution. As a result, it was destined to attract many others who fled from religious persecution from Europe, especially from the area that is now Germany. Today we know the offspring of these particular settlers as the Pennsylvania Dutch. Among them were highly skilled gunsmiths, and they and their successors developed the extremely accurate Long Rifle, which played a crucial role before and after the American Revolution in the westward expansion of the original thirteen colonies. Because of the part it played on the frontier, it came to be known as the Kentucky Rifle, but it was the product of the genius of Swiss and German gunsmiths in Pennsylvania.

The Royal Charter in which Charles II gave land to William Penn also opened a vast new territory where beavers, otters, and other valuable fur-bearers were abundant. Pelts could easily be brought downriver to the excellent port at Philadelphia where they could be shipped to England. During their tenure, the Dutch had not been able to exploit this resource as they had done in New York. It is one of the great ironies of history that of all the thirteen English colonies in North America, the one founded upon the principle of peace, brotherly love, and good will toward men was destined to be the one in which war was started. It was in Pennsylvania that the soldiers of France ambushed an army composed of British regulars and armed colonials.

Britain was no less intolerant of those who did not conform to the doctrine of the state church than was France. However, Britain's policy was more practical and proved to be more profitable. France refused to let the Huguenots settle in New France, and instead she massacred, imprisoned, and waged a costly war against them. Britain, on the other hand, permitted the Puritans to settle in New England, the Quakers in Pennsylvania, and the Catholics in Maryland.

In 1631, Britain granted land to Cecilius Calvert, Lord Baltimore, as a refuge for British Catholics and others who sought religious freedom. His brother led two hundred settlers to Mary's River in 1634.

In addition to those who wished to escape religious persecution, there were others who had every reason to emigrate and seek a new life. It was the law of the land in England at the time to arrest and put in prison those who were unable to pay their debts. Unless some wealthy friend or relative discharged those debts, this was tantamount to life imprisonment for being unfortunate, improvident, or a combination thereof. Those who wrote the law failed to take into consideration the fact that when a man is in prison for debt, he is unable to pay it. Moreover, while he is there, he is an item of public expense.

Because of this condition, General James Oglethorpe received a land grant from England, and in 1633, he landed in Savannah with colonists and founded the Georgia colony. These were free men, but Georgia was organized as a refuge for poor Englishmen and those who wished to have religious freedom. The colony did not go unchallenged for Spain had also laid claim to the territory, and in 1642, Oglethorpe fought and defeated a Spanish army from Florida at Bloody Marsh.

All these colonies had excellent harbors from which beaver pelts and other furs could be shipped to England. In the north, Britain was shipping them out of Hudson Bay from the Hudson's Bay Company's posts, while France was restricted largely to exporting furs out of the St. Lawrence River.

England established colonies along the east coast from New England on the north to Spanish territory in Florida on the south, but while she was doing it, the Swedes had landed and established colonies in Delaware in 1638 and Pennsylvania in 1643.

The Dutch became firmly established in the area that is now New York State. In 1614 and again in 1624, they established a trading post near present day Albany. It was known as Fort Orange, and they were actively engaged in fur-trading with the Indians. In 1626, the Dutch settled on Manhattan Island, and in 1664, with a force of three hundred soldiers, the British took it over from Peter Stuyvesant, who had no force to oppose them. King Charles II gave the territory to his brother James, Duke of York, and named it New York. At the same time that New York was taken over, so were the settlements of the Dutch in Pennsylvania, Delaware, and New Jersey, leaving the English in complete domination of the east coast from New England to Spanish Florida.

The Beaver Fur Trade in the Northeastern United States and Eastern Canada

Very soon after settlers landed, they became active in the beaver trade. Babcock (2) stated,

> No animal has been so closely associated with, and instrumental in the development of New England as the beaver. Its pelt at once became the unit of trade between Colonies and Indians, and remained so for many years, while on the other hand the colonies shipped thousands of beaver skins to England, annually, which were received instead of gold in payment of debts. . . We find the Plymouth Colony almost immediately engaging with the Indians in trade for beaver.

In fact, the trade in furs began with the first meeting with the Indians at Patuxet (New Plymouth) at which Samoset was urged on his first visit to bring in neighboring Indians, "with such beaver skins as they had to trade." Later, trade with the Massachusetts Bay and surrounding tribes was organized through Massasoit and Tisquantum, and beaver skins constituted the basis for all exchange. This trade often proved a source of competition and strife, not only among individuals, but also among several colonies as border disputes arose in connection with fur-trade activities.

In Plymouth after the first hard winter was over and the supply of corn assured, the settlers found time to develop fur trade with the Indians. Bradford (11) speaks of an exploring party sent out in 1621 which brought back a good quantity of beaver skins. In 1626, after the harvest, they began trading with the Indians at "Kenebeck," sending out a boatload of corn and bringing home "700 li" of beaver and other furs.

The returns of the beaver trade between 1631 and 1636 amounted to about ten thousand pounds sterling for the Plymouth Plantation alone, which more than paid the debts of the colony.

Babcock (2) also wrote, ". . . by 1764 very few beaver were being turned in to the Massachusetts Treasury by the Truckmasters and the price had dropped. From this time, the beavers as an important factor of trade in New England (except Maine) ceased to exist."

Some very interesting information concerning the beaver trade in New York is found in the reports written by James T. DeKay (5) in 1842:

> The beaver whose skins once formed so important an article of commerce to this state have been incorporated into the armorial bearings of the old colony is now nearly extirpated within its limits. The skins of this animal even constituted a certain standard of value, and were a portion of the circulating medium. Thus, in 1697, we find that Governor Fletcher made a certain grant of a tract of land on the Mohawk and the consideration named in the deed was one beaver skin for the first year and five forever after.

> According to a letter from the Dutch West India Company, which is preserved in the Albany records, we learn that in 1624, 400 beaver and 700 otter skins were exported. The number increased in 1635 to 14,891 beaver and 1,413 otter skins, and that the whole number in the ten years was 80,183 beavers and 7,347 otters, amounting in value to 725,117 Guilders. In the same letter, the directors complain that beavers have become exceedingly scarce; having been sold at seven Guilders a piece, and even more. One of the earliest legislative enactments by the rulers of the colony was in reference to the peltry trade; and I notice in the same records alluded to above, William DeKay, an ancestor of the writer, was appointed receiver of the duties on beaver and bear skins.

> I am informed by T.O. Fowler that in 1815 a party of St. Regis Indians from Canada ascended the Oeswegatchie River in the County of St. Lawrence in pursuit of beaver. In consequence of the hostilities between this country and England, this district had not been hunted for some years and the beaver had consequently been undisturbed. The party after an absence of a few weeks returned with three hundred beaver skins. These were seen by my informant, who adds that since that time very few have been observed.

Quoting DeKay, Morgan (14) wrote:

> Each pelt was then worth about two dollars and a quarter. The trade steadily increased until the domination of the Dutch ended in 1664. Beaver pelts were then a measure of value and formed a part of the currency; and the beaver himself was adopted for the central

symbol of the seal of the province. Their fur continued, under English rule to be the chief article of export from New York until 1700, after which the exportation declined rapidly and soon became extinct. In 1687, Thomas Dongan, Governor of the Province of New York, remarked in a letter as follows. "We find that the revenue is very much diminished, for in other years we used to ship off to England thirty-five to forty thousand beaver, besides peltry. This year only nine thousands some hundreds, peltry and all." Again in November 1700, Governor Belmont wrote to the Lords of Trade in equally discouraging language. "The beaver trade here and at Boston has shrunk to little or nothing, and the market is so low for beaver in England that it is scarce worth the transporting." I have been told that in one year, when the province was in possession of the Dutch, that there were sixty-six thousand beaver skins transported from this town, and that last year there were but fifteen thousand, two hundred and forty-one exported hence.

When the Dutch sent settlers to the New World, they found themselves in an area where beavers and other fur-bearers were plentiful. They were quick to exploit this opportunity. Six years before the Pilgrims landed at Plymouth, the Dutch built a trading post at the site of present-day Albany, which became Fort Orange. This was the collecting point for furs taken in the western and central areas of the colony that were brought down the Mohawk as well as those taken in Canada and the Adirondack region that were brought down the Hudson. New Amsterdam was also a strategic location for furs taken in the Catskill region and New Jersey. Ships could sail up the Hudson River as far as Fort Orange, take aboard a load of furs, and sail down river to New Amsterdam to pick up additional cargo bound for Amsterdam.

A well-traveled north-south trade route developed. The headwaters of the Upper Hudson are not far from Lake George, and the upper end of Lake George is not far from the south end of Lake Champlain. Except for these two portages and the one around Glens Falls, there is a water route that can be traveled by canoe from the St. Lawrence down to New York Harbor. The French had used it to transport furs north out of New England and upper New York, and the Dutch and later the English used it to transfer furs south.

The Dutch had an added advantage: the Indians were eager to trade with them. At the time a number of tribes of Indians inhabited the New York colony, but the most powerful group was the Confederation of the Iroquois. Of all the eastern Indians, they had the most highly developed social system. They lived in settled communities and were no longer dependent upon food gathering, hunting, and fishing for survival. As successful farmers they raised corn, beans, squash, and gourds. After European contact, they added fruit trees, and when they secured the appropriate tools, they abandoned the long house for log cabins, some with glass windows. There were five tribes at the time: the Senecas, the Cayugas, the Onondagas, the Oneidas, and the Mohawks. The Tuscoraras joined the confederacy later.

The Iroquois occupied some of the most fertile land and best hunting and fishing grounds in eastern North America, and they were ready and able to defend it. The greatest threat of invasion was from the north. The central tribes, the Cayugas, the Onondagas, and the Oneidas, had Lake Ontario that provided considerable protection. The ends of the lake were most vulnerable to war parties, and the most powerful, most warlike nations were positioned to protect these potential invasion routes. The Senecas were designated as "Keepers of the Western Gate" to prevent attacks from the Niagara region, and similarly the Mohawks at the eastern end of the lake were expected to prevent attacks from across the St. Lawrence.

As a result of their experience with Champlain at Ticonderoga, the Iroquois viewed the French and their allies as their enemies. They had learned that firearms can kill at a greater distance than their native weapons and thus wished to possess and learn to use them. They were eventually successful on both counts.

The Dutch found the Indians eager to exchange beaver pelts for trade goods. Very high on the list of things they desired were firearms and ammunition, and they made full use of them in both hunting and warfare. From the time the Dutch built the trading post at Fort Orange until the British wrested the colony from Holland in 1664, they had a near monopoly of the lucrative fur trade in the colony. The Iroquois were a most effective barrier against the French and Algonquin penetration from the north.

From the time England took over the Dutch colonies, she had complete control over settlements from Florida north. Coastal communities grew at a rapid pace, and from them pioneering groups rapidly moved inland, cleared the land, and established new communities. In so doing, they created conditions where the beaver could no longer exist. Nevertheless, beaver pelts were still a very important item of trade. Bales of skins were shipped out of the harbors of Charlestown, Savannah, Philadelphia, New York, and Boston, but the English colonies were also exporting them with another item of trade, tobacco. The demand for beaver skins was unabated, but it was necessary to go farther and farther inland to get them. While English colonists were moving farther north to get beaver skins, those who were marketing their catches with Hudson's Bay Company were moving farther south for the same purpose.

The French were being ground between the upper and nether millstones, and they responded by building forts at Ticonderoga and at the mouth of the Niagara River, and they maintained garrisons of French troops in them. French troops and Algonquin allies conducted armed expeditions south in attempts to crush the Iroquois. The one direction in which they could expand their fur trade was to the west, the Upper Great Lakes, the Ohio region, and down the Mississippi River.

The beaver was the unwitting cause of a series of events that brought France and England on to a collision course. Disputes over territory and the fur trade erupted into intermittent armed conflicts that escalated until they culminated in a long and bloody war that pitted armies of French soldiers and their Indian allies against those of Britain, combined with American colonists and her Indian allies in a struggle to determine which country would control the trade and dominate eastern North America.

By the middle of the eighteenth century, the French population in Canada numbered between 50,000 and 60,000 fur traders and farmers. They were outnumbered twenty to one by English colonists spread out along the east coast from Georgia on the south to Newfoundland on the north. Britain at the time also possessed superior sea power.

War between France and England could have been started at any place along the borders, but it started when young George Washington was sent out on an expedition by Governor Dinwiddie of Virginia. He found that the French were building forts along the entire Ohio River Valley. Washington was sent out again in 1754, at which time he found that the French had built Fort Duquense at the confluence of the Allegheny and Monongahela Rivers. He was defeated at Great Meadows and forced to retreat. The French were firmly in control and could only be dislodged by a strong military expedition. In 1755, General Edward Braddock headed a campaign to capture the fort with an army of British regulars and Virginians under Washington. They were ambushed about eight miles from the fort by French and Indians and defeated with heavy loss of life to the British regulars, and in the engagement Braddock was killed.

Neither England nor France wanted a full-scale war three thousand miles away, since each was involved on opposite sides in a full-scale war in Europe. Both hoped that it could be confined locally. Nevertheless, with the defeat of Braddock they were propelled into a bitter conflict that would drag on for years, involving not only the armies and navies of France and England but colonists and Indians as well.

In the early days, despite superior numbers, things did not go well for the English and her allies. There were numerous raids by the French and their Indian allies against western settlements in Pennsylvania, Maryland, and Virginia, and England's forces suffered costly defeats with heavy losses. It was not until 1758 that the tide began to turn. The English forces recaptured Louisburg, and George Washington, on the staff of General John Forbes, was involved in the capture of Fort Duquense. The defeat of Montcalm by General Wolfe on the Plains of Abraham and capture of Quebec by English forces in 1759 and the capture of Montreal in 1760 gave England control of the Great Lakes and the entire St. Lawrence River. The Treaty of Paris signed in February 1763 gave to England all of Canada and the lands east of the Mississippi except New Orleans.

Seven years of warfare that had been waged on two continents and the high seas had cost England heavily. It is one of the ironies of history that in attempting to pay for her involvement, England instituted a policy that was destined to involve her in yet another seven-year war in North America that would be far more costly. The east coast colonies at the time were thirteen separate political entities, each with its own laws and regulations. Between them there were disagreements, jealousies, and even acts of hostility. Nevertheless, this most unlikely group of highly individualistic states was destined to become a sovereign nation. England turned to her colonies as a source of revenue and levied a series of taxes that were so bitterly resented by the colonists that armed rebellion broke out in Massachusetts in 1775, resulting in a full-scale war. George Washington was named General of the Continental Army. The war dragged on for seven years and finally was brought to an end with the help of France and Spain.

The Treaty of Paris in 1782 gave the thirteen colonies their freedom and all the land east of the Mississippi, but there was still another war to be fought before fur traders from Hudson's Bay Company could be dislodged from their posts on the south sides of the Great Lakes and the United States would have the undisputed rights to travel on the Great Lakes.

In colonial times population in the settlements doubled every generation, with the most rapid growth rates in New England where the rate of survival for children born was possibly the highest in history. There, the rocky country with its thin soil was ill-fitted to support the rapidly expanding population. Before the Revolutionary War, the Iroquois with English protection effectively blocked western expansion. During the war, two bloody raids were carried out by the Iroquois in Cherry Valley and Wyoming Valley. In retaliation, General Washington organized an expedition under Generals James Clinton and John Sullivan in 1779 that destroyed the villages of the Onondaga, Cayuga, and Seneca and burned their crops. This expedition effectively destroyed the power of the Iroquois. After the war in 1797, at the present site of Geneseo, New York, the Treaty of Big Tree was signed. The Senecas surrendered claim to most of their land for what amounted to a few cents per acre. The last barrier to western expansion was removed.

The Beaver Fur Trade in the Western United States

Among the soldiers in the Sullivan Expedition were a number from New England. They were greatly impressed with the country occupied by the Iroquois, and they returned home with glowing tales to tell about the fertile land in central and western New York. After the signing of the Treaty of Big Tree, many of them with their families were among the tide of New Englanders who moved west to settle this country. This had once been prime beaver country. Some of the settlers found land in stream valleys where many generations of beavers had maintained ponds that had acted as settling basins for silt and organic matter. In those places the soil was richest and deepest.

Except for occasional clearings, the country was covered with a stand of magnificent hardwoods, some of them centuries old. Their value today would be many times more than that of the land upon which they stood. Thousands of acres of these trees were cut down and burned to clear the land, and this was in addition to those cut for building material, fences, and firewood. Later waves of settlers repeated the process in Ohio and Indiana. Immediately after the Revolutionary War, settlers also moved into Kentucky and Tennessee with equally destructive practices.

The settlers moved in, cleared, and occupied land that had once been prime beaver country, but even before they arrived, the beaver population had been severely depleted. A combination of ruthless killing and destruction of habitat soon eliminated the beaver from any area that man had cleared and settled. The Beaver was not the only creature affected. By 1830, the Woodland Bison, Woodland Caribou, Moose, Whitetail Deer, Cougar, Wolf, Wolverine, Fisher, Marten, Otter, Wild Turkey, Bobcat, Snowshoe Hare, and Ruffed Grouse had almost completely disappeared. The Red Fox, Raccoon, and even the Gray Squirrel were seldom seen. The only exceptions were in wilderness areas that were deliberately avoided because the hillsides were too steep and the soil too thin.

At the beginning of the nineteenth century the beaver had disappeared from most areas in the thirteen original states and was becoming increasingly scarce in eastern and central Canada as well. However, west of the Mississippi was a vast area that trappers had seldom penetrated, and the beaver population was enormous. Within a relatively short time, a number of events combined to trigger an explosive migration of settlers traveling west. In less than half a

The first white men to explore the far west found great mountain valleys like this one entirely filled with active beaver ponds. In addition to many beaver, there was an abundance of fish, waterfowl, and animals thriving on the lush conditions created by the beaver. These ponds in Grand Teton National Park are now abandoned, but give us a good idea of the extensive beaver ponds of the past.

A cow moose with calf feeding in an immense beaver meadow in the Rockies as these are doing would have been a common sight for the first white trappers of the early 1800s.

century, the United States of America expanded from thirteen states along the eastern seaboard to a mighty nation occupying the center of North America from the Atlantic to the Pacific.

In 1803, during Thomas Jefferson's administration, the Louisiana Purchase was completed, and this more than doubled the area of the United States. In the years 1804–1806, the Lewis and Clark Expedition explored the country that had just been purchased and that lay to the west. They did not turn back until they reached the Pacific Ocean. The expedition stimulated interest in the lands that lay to the west, but of special interest were their stories about the abundance of the beaver.

In the early years of the reign of George IV, Beau Brummel was the style setter for what the well-dressed English gentleman would wear. The clothes he wore were imitated by men who could afford them across Europe and America. He was responsible for the popularity of the "gray beaver," the hat that rapidly became the hallmark of the well-attired male. Up until that time there had been a very active demand for beaver fur to make hats. With the popularity of the gray beaver there was a sudden and dramatic increase in the demand for beaver skins.

In the United States a number of fur companies merged to form the American Fur Company, which was headed by John Jacob Astor. In 1811, he founded Astoria on the south bank of the Columbia River as a depot for Indian, Alaskan, and Russian fur trade. It was captured by the British in 1812, but was later restored. On the basis of the settlement, Astoria, the United States laid claim to the Oregon Territory.

Until 1823, beavers were generally killed according to the methods that had been developed by the Indians. They were slower and involved a considerable amount of physical effort, but they were effective. One method was to make certain that the animals were in a bank burrow. Then stakes were driven into the bottom of the pond to block the exits. When that was done, the den was dug out, and the beavers were killed. When the pond was frozen over, a double row of stakes was driven to form a long corridor through which beavers were forced to leave or enter the house. Near the house a hole was cut through the ice and a twig placed in it. When a beaver left the house, it moved the twig, but before it could return, a heavy stake was driven into the pond bottom. When the beaver returned, it could not come up for air, and it drowned. Then a hole was chopped through the ice, and the dead beaver was removed. In 1823, Sewell Newhouse of Oneida, New York, invented a new device for taking and killing not only beavers, but all other fur-bearers as well: the steel trap.

When steel traps became available, trappers could carry three or four dozen with them. Instead of concentrating on taking one beaver at a time, he "ran a trap line." This he did by setting traps in strategic locations over as large a territory as he could cover in a day, with the result that he could take as many animals on a single trip as he could possibly skin and care for.

This happened at the time when there was the greatest demand for beaver fur to make the gray beaver hat. The result was a sudden and drastic decrease in the numbers of beavers and increasing pressure on those that had managed to survive.

In "The Beaver," Bert Grescham (7) gave some interesting information concerning the effectiveness of traps.

> For instance we might study the narrative by James O. Pattre, who tells of trapping 450 beaver from December 1824 to March 1825 in Arizona. In one night with forty traps, he and his party captured thirty-six beaver and records the fact that catches of sixty a day were sometimes made. Those were the days when fur traders put seventy or eighty pelts in a 100–pound bale and sold them for from $3.00 to $4.00 per pound in St. Louis. Often the skins were bought from the Indians for a few cents worth of trade goods. Alexander Ross, a member of the J. J. Astor expedition which founded Astoria in the early nineteenth century, tells of buying one hundred and ten beaver skins at Fort Kamploops for five leaves of tobacco per skin, but he made a better bargain when he got twenty prime beaver skins from the chief for his last remaining yard of white cotton.
>
> In those days, beaver was of such vast importance that the beaver pelt was literally the currency of the fur trade. Other furs and articles of merchandise were valued at so many beaver pelts, and it followed as a matter of course that man-made tokens were used in trading. By the middle of the nineteenth century, trade in beaver pelts reached staggering figures, and between 1853 and 1877, the Hudson's Bay Company sold 2,965,389 skins at the London Market. In the year 1867 alone, the Company sold 172,042 pelts to set what is probably the maximum sales record.

In addition to the instances which Grescham mentioned, there are multitudes of other tales concerning traders' dealings with the Indians and the prices that were paid in beaver pelts for trade goods. One that has had wide circulation is the price the Indian paid for a gun in some instances. He was required to pay for it with a stack of beaver pelts as high as the length of the gun. If the new owner found that it was longer than he liked, he could have it shortened by the company blacksmith by paying for his work with a stack of pelts as high as the piece that was cut off. This was hardly a "Pro Pelle Cutem" arrangement.

The years of the heyday of the western beaver trade were boom times for many traders and some of the successful trappers. Several hundred dollars could sometimes be made in a single week and a fortune could be made in a single season. We can get an idea of the purchasing power of money during the period from the records of a district school in the Town of Parma, Monroe County, New York, during that period, which reads: "We, the trustees have resolved to appropriate the sum of five hundred dollars to operate the school during the coming year, including the teacher's wages."

At the time the fur trade was expanding westward on land, there was a new development in the fur trade off the west coast. In 1741, Vitus Bering, a Danish explorer, was the first European to land in Alaska. He led an expedition financed by Russia and on the basis of his discovery, Russia laid claim to the territory. The report of the abundance of fur seals and sea otters attracted huge numbers of sealers and hunters which resulted in a wholesale slaughter of fur-bearing animals to the point where they soon became exceedingly rare. As a result, the hunting of sea otters moved down the coast off California. Russians were not the only ones involved, but their numbers predominated. They had settlements in Alaska and along the coast that were their bases of operation. As a result of the unrestricted killing, the Alaskan Sea Otter became a very rare animal, the fur seal was in danger of extinction, and for many years the California Sea Otter was thought to be extinct.

This activity off the coast did not go unnoticed in California. There was serious concern in Spain and in California that Russia or England would occupy the land. As a counter measure the Franciscan Father Sierra Juniper founded the Alta California Mission at San Diego in 1769, and from there added new missions and settlements up the coast to San Francisco for the dual purpose of converting the Indians to Christianity and preventing Russian and English settlements along the coast. The missions were spaced approximately thirty-five miles apart, the average distance that could be traveled in a day. Around each mission communities rapidly sprang up. The string of missions which he founded have been referred to as the beads on Father Juniper's rosary. They were successful in preventing the colonization by Russia or England, but they could not stem the tide of American trappers, traders, and adventurers that rolled in from the east. Farther north, following the trails of the trappers, wagon trains were rolling west carrying settlers to occupy the Oregon Territory.

While trappers combed the headwaters of western rivers in quest of beaver pelts, in New England shipbuilders were constructing fleets of the swiftest ocean going vessels the world had ever seen. These were the sleek and beautiful clipper ships that sailed the Seven Seas carrying merchandise to and from ports in North America and the markets of the world. This was the heyday for the clipper ship and the Yankee trader.

It was also the golden era of the China trade. Furs from America were in great demand by the wealthy Chinese. From the east coast beaver pelts and other furs were chief items of export as were the roots of a plant that grew wild in the eastern woodlands, ginseng. The Chinese prized it for its reputed medicinal properties. The skin of the sea otter commanded the highest price of any fur. From the west coast ports, clipper ships carried otter skins and other furs, including beaver skins, to the ports of China, and they returned home with tea, silks, spices, and the exquisite porcelain which we know as china. For this there was a ready market among the rapidly growing wealthy class of Americans.

Unprecedented demand for beaver skins to make hats plus their increasing importance as items of export in the rapidly expanding China trade drove the prices paid per skin to record levels. The steel trap made it possible for a trapper to greatly increase the number of fur-bearers he could take during a trapping season. This whole set of circumstances could have only one result: a mass assault upon the beavers in the few remote areas where they were still plentiful.

During the first four decades of the nineteenth century, more beaver skins were probably shipped out per year than at any time in history. Competition between Hudson's Bay Company and the American Fur Company was fierce, and it sometimes resulted in armed conflict. The same situation existed among free traders, between individual trappers, trappers and Indians, Indians and Indians. No claim to territory was honored unless it could be held by force.

John Jacob Astor cornered the nation's fur trade, created the first trust, helped finance the War of 1812, was a friend of presidents, was one of the founders of the Second Bank of the United States, and built what is said to be the greatest American fortune of his day. He was born near Heidelberg, Germany, July 17, 1763, and left Germany for London when he was sixteen to work in his brother's piano and flute factory. In 1783, he emigrated to the United States to be an agent in his brother's firm, Astor and Broadwood. Two years later, Astor traveled up the Hudson to trade in furs, and by the mid-1790s, he had become one of the leading fur merchants in the United States. Through friendship with a London official of the East India Company, Astor obtained a charter authorizing him to trade freely with any port monopolized by the company. This opened the way for Astor's transactions with China, then the richest fur market. He founded his own shipping company to carry his furs to Canton, St. Petersburg, and London.

In 1808, he was appointed executive officer by President Jefferson and organized the American Fur Company to challenge the North West Company and Hudson's Bay Company. In 1811, while organizing the Pacific Fur Company, he founded Astoria, the first American permanent settlement in the Pacific Northwest. In 1822, the pressure of private companies led by Astor and his American Fur Company induced Congress to abandon the government program of maintaining trading posts. Astor took over the smaller companies, and by 1827, he had a monopoly on the export of furs from the United States and was strong enough to challenge Hudson's Bay Company. This string of trading posts or forts provided protection for the transfer of furs and merchandise, and they also played a most important role as protection and supply stations when the wagon trains with settlers were moving west. However, they were in fixed positions that were sometimes long distances from the places where trappers operated.

One of the first men to explore the Rocky Mountains in quest of beaver skins was John Colter. In 1803, he enlisted in the army to join the Lewis and Clark Expedition. He stayed with the surveying party until it was homeward bound, but at a Mandan Indian village in North Dakota, he turned westward in the company of two white trappers and spent more years in the wilderness. In 1807, he accompanied the trader, Manuel Lisa, up the Missouri on a trading expedition across the

These old beaver ponds in Yellowstone National Park were built long ago by several generations of beavers over a period of many years.

mountain ranges of Wyoming to the Yellowstone National Park region. There he met with a number of adventures. One that he related concerned a party of Blackfoot Indians on the warpath who were after his scalp. He eluded them and saved his life by crawling into a beaver house. The stories he told about Yellowstone and its natural wonders found few believers. They referred to the area he described as "Colter's Hell." One who did believe him was his old commander, William Clark. Colter gave Clark valuable geographical information on his return.

On March 6, 1822, William Henry Ashley and his partner, Andrew Henry, advertised in the *Missouri Democrat* for one hundred enterprising young men to ascend the Missouri to its source, there to be employed for one, two, or three years. A group of young men headed by Jedediah Strong Smith and James Bridger responded to Ashley's call. Other famous trappers who got their start with Ashley were William and Milton Sublette, David Jackson, from whom Jackson Hole, Wyoming gets its name, and Etiénne Provost. From him, the city of Provo, Utah received its name.

Mountain Men

In 1825, General William H. Ashley initiated a most important departure from the fixed trading posts. For a period of fifteen years, trappers and Indians gathered by previous arrangement in a certain valley. There they were met by the caravans of traders from the settlements. A gathering of this type was known as a "rendezvous." The places usually selected could be reached by wagon trains rather than pack mules. The traders brought supplies directly to the areas that were convenient to trappers and saved them long distances of travel to the trading posts. Firearms, powder, lead, axes, knives, traps, cloth, salt, tea, coffee, and other items that would be needed during the next season in the wilderness were sold to trappers, and when they became available, most certainly steel traps became important items of trade. Sometimes they were exchanged by barter, but they were also issued on credit as an advance against the next year's catch of furs. Occasionally they were bought outright or by issue of drafts against banks in St. Louis. Some of the trappers were independent operators while others were employees of the traders, but these men freely switched allegiance to whichever company gave the best deal at the time. High on the list of desired trade goods were glass beads, mirrors, tacks, and the like. Indians were soon stripped of their valuables for goods of little worth.

The rendezvous lasted a few days or a few weeks. Wherever they were held, they had one thing in common. Whiskey was brought in as a chief article of trade, but it was rarely if ever the pure article. As a result these gatherings were prolonged periods of debauchery, fraud, treachery, and bloodshed.

The trappers who attended these gatherings and similar events at the trading posts became known as the "mountain men." Their numbers probably never exceeded fifteen hundred, but from about 1805 to 1840, they explored every mountain pass and every watercourse to its headwaters in quest of beaver skins.

The mountain men were forced to adapt to a set of conditions far different and often more severe than those encountered by the trapper in the eastern woodlands, especially in travel and transportation. His eastern counterpart could travel and transport materials long distances by lightweight birch-bark canoe. The mountain man did not have the materials to build one, and there were very few places where it could be used. As a result, he relied upon the horse and sometimes the mule for transportation. He had at least two horses, one to ride and the other to carry his equipment, which included pots and pans for cooking, food, blankets, lead, a bullet mold, extra powder, traps, and the like. He always carried a rifle; if possible, it was one of the type made by the famous gunsmith Hawkin of St. Louis. Used against the grizzly and other large animals of the west, it required a much larger and heavier bullet than the one used in the Kentucky rifle carried by Daniel Boone and the other frontiersmen of his generation. Slung from his shoulder was a powder horn and carried on his belt was a "Green River" knife, possibly a pipe and tobacco pouch, and always a flint and steel for making fire.

His dress and personal appearance were dictated to a large extent by his way of life in the wilderness. It was a harsh existence that afforded little time or opportunity for personal grooming. When he came out at the end of a trapping season, he was usually unshaved, unshorn, and unkempt, bearded and with long hair hanging loose around his shoulders except when there was an Indian wife to carefully braid it. His head was usually covered with a felt hat with a fairly wide brim; lacking that he might be wearing one made from the skin of a raccoon or other fur-bearing animal. He sometimes wore clothing made from blankets, especially from Hudson's Bay Company point blankets if they were available. Pants and shirts were among the items he obtained from traders.

Fringed buckskin garments and leggings were common. The fringe was not intended as ornamentation; a wet garment that was fringed dried faster. On his feet, he wore moccasins. During periods of forced idleness over the course of long winter months, he often made for himself the items of clothing necessary to survive.

The mountain man, of necessity, traveled light and was out of contact with sources of supplies from the beginning of the trapping

87

season in the fall until he came out with his load of furs in the spring. He seldom stayed long in one place. As soon as he had trapped out the beavers in one area, he moved on to find a new one where they were still plentiful. Under the best of conditions, he had little opportunity to set up a main camp where he had proper shelter. He also operated in places where whether he lived or died depended upon his ability to find a safe hiding place to sleep each night and to avoid detection during the day. He was sometimes in the vicinity of Blackfoot warriors who were eager to lift his scalp. There were also elements of his own kind, ever ready to rob him of his possessions and having no compunction against killing him to get them. There was also constant danger from the forces of nature. He lived in a world where there was no law; it did not exist beyond the settlements.

After animals were taken, there was much work to be done. To remove the hide from a beaver, the animal was laid on its back and a slit made down the belly from chin to the base of the tail. Then cuts across were made from the center cut to the ends of the legs. When the skin was removed, the first operation was to clean it of all flesh and fat: a critical and difficult operation, but a well-prepared skin brought a higher price. The next operation was to fasten it to a hoop made of bent willow. The skins were dried on these frames until they were "cured" and ready to be removed and stored.

Beaver skins were graded for size as well as quality, and they fell roughly into three groups: yearlings, two-year-olds, and adults. The most valuable was a large skin of high quality. One that measured sixty inches or more across when stretched was known as a blanket beaver, or a plus, and it became a standard of value in trade. A skin measuring seventy inches or over was graded as a super blanket. Tokens representing beaver skins were freely circulated. Beavers were skinned "open." Muskrat, mink, and marten skins were "cased." Skinning was done by making cuts across the back legs at the base of the tail. The skin was removed by turning it inside out. When this was done and the skin was "fleshed," it was stretched over a piece of willow bent into the shape of a "U."

The mountain man added a new word to the English vocabulary, *cache*. What he could not carry or wished to conceal he cached by digging a pit large enough to hold the furs or other possessions for hiding. He roofed it over with saplings or small logs and covered them with earth in such a way that his possessions were safe from detection by man or beast. These caches were often made in the fall, and the locations were concealed by a covering of snow, leaving the contents in cold storage during the winter months. In the spring when he was ready to take his furs out to market, he opened the caches and removed them.

Methods of transporting furs out to market depended upon the topography of the land and the resources of the trapper. In most areas it was done by pack horses or mule train, and in some areas by wagon train. The first wagons to reach the mountains were those of the Smith, Jackson, Sublette Fur Trading Expedition, which exploited the rich Jackson Hole country. They went by way of the Platte River and Scott's Bluff: the route eventually called the Oregon Trail.

At the points of assembly, skins were put in crude presses and baled so that they would occupy less space. A "pack" of furs contained usually ten buffalo robes, fourteen bear skins, eighty beaver or six hundred muskrat skins. Where water transportation was possible, the bull boat was often used. A clumsy craft, the frame was a basket-like structure made of willow or some other flexible wood. Over it was stretched a covering of untanned buffalo hides. It could carry up to two tons and was of shallow draft, well adapted to shallow rivers like the Platte. It was vulnerable to snags and sand bars, however, and dugout canoes hacked out of single cottonwood logs were sometimes used on smaller streams. These capsized with irritating frequency.

In the valley of the Missouri River, downstream transportation was often by keel boats. These had to be either poled or pulled by groups of from twenty to forty men along the shore. Flat-bottomed mackinaw boats were also used for downstream transportation. The final stretch of downstream transportation of these packs of furs was accomplished by steamboat.

The era of the mountain man was roughly between the years 1822 and 1840, the year that a hatter's apprentice in London discovered that chopped silk fibers make more lustrous hats than those made from the fur of the beaver. The silk top hat immediately became the item of headgear worn by the well-dressed man, and it quickly supplanted the gray beaver that was made popular by Beau Brummel earlier in the century. As a result, the bottom dropped out of the market for beaver skins; these had been the backbone of the mountain and western fur trade. Years of relentless trapping had exterminated the beaver in areas where it had once been abundant, and the beaver was a very rare creature in the few places where it had managed to survive. This scarcity combined with very low prices discouraged the mountain man from making dangerous trips into the wilderness. The era of the mountain men lasted less than two decades, but because of them, no area so vast has ever been explored so thoroughly and so fast. They came to know every watercourse and every mountain opening through which wagon trains could pass.

Their numbers were never great but the part that mountain men played in the exploration and development of the continent and their impact on the environment was far out of proportion to their numbers.

Within a few years they reduced the beaver population to the point where it became a threatened species. In the process these men also eliminated the ponds the beavers had maintained, disrupted the lives, and decimated the numbers of creatures that used his ponds and clearings. The absence of the beaver upset the delicate balance of Nature that had evolved over thousands of years.

When the boom period of the beaver trade ended in 1840, the importance of the mountain men and traders continued. Their knowledge of the country and of the Indians and their customs was of greatest importance during the following period of trade and travel. Former mountain men guided wagon trains to Oregon, California, and Utah. Some acted as scouts for the United States Cavalry in campaigns against the Indians. At least one former mountain man served as an Indian agent and was well-known for his enlightened administration. Some who were involved in the fur trade amassed fortunes, and others were elected to important offices in both the United States and Canada.

One of the most skillful and dependable American frontiersmen was Colonel Christopher "Kit" Carson. He grew up in Missouri in an atmosphere of Indian fighting. At age 15 he was apprenticed to a saddle maker but ran away. In 1828 he joined a party to make his first trip to Sante Fe and California. In 1830 he joined another party into the Central Rocky Mountains whre he spent twelve eventful years as a Mountain Man. He married an Indian girl who bore him a daughter. During the Mexican War he seved the army as a guide and scout. In 1842 and 1843 he served as guide and counselor to Lieutenant John Charles Freemont on his first two expeditions. During the Civil War from 1862 to 1864 he conducted campaigns agains the Comanches, Kiowas, Apaches and Navajoes. After the war he served briefly as Brevet Brigadier General at Fort Garland, Colorado. He died at Fort Lyon, Colorado, May 13, 1868.

Nine years after the beginning of the decline of the fur trade, gold was discovered in California. The prospectors and adventurers who traveled from the east and became known as "The Forty-Niners" followed the routes previously discovered by the mountain men in their quest for riches in the form of the soft fur of the beaver.

3

Restoration of the Beaver Population

As trappers eliminated the beaver in one area, they moved on to others where they were still plentiful. When they came out to sell their furs or get supplies, they often told tales about the fertile lands that they had explored. As a result, the trappers were soon followed by a tide of settlers that rolled inland from coastal settlements and westward from New England. They cut down trees, cleared the land, and built dams on streams and rivers to turn water wheels. As communities sprang up along the watercourses, the streams became polluted with sewage and industrial wastes. Within a generation millions of acres of prime beaver habitat had been destroyed.

The Beaver was not the only living thing to suffer from the advance of man. By 1830, the Woodland Bison, Elk, Moose, Woodland Caribou, Black Bear, Timber Wolf, Cougar, Otter, Fisher, Marten, Wolverine, and Wild Turkey had also either disappeared or existed in very small numbers in eastern North America. The Whitetail Deer, Raccoon, Bobcat, and even the Gray Squirrel were creatures that were seldom seen.

There were still areas that had been bypassed by the tide of settlers because the terrain was too rugged, the growing seasons too short, or both. They were still covered with stands of magnificent trees. These "inexhaustible" stands of timber were viewed with keen interest by the timber barons. They started in Maine and worked their way west across northern New England, the Adirondack regions of New York, then to Michigan, Wisconsin, and Minnesota. Farther north, the process was repeated in Canada. Within a generation most of the prime timber in the eastern states and eastern Canada had been logged off. The "cut-and-move-on" tactics left behind immense areas of stump land devoid of timber and unsuited for agriculture. After they had logged off the eastern part of the continent, the lumber barons moved their operations to the west coast.

In spite of the reduced demand for the making of hats, the fur of the beaver was still in demand for other purposes, and the killing continued. It appeared that the Beaver was destined to share the fate of the Passenger Pigeon, the Carolina Parakeet, Labrador Duck, and the Heath Hen. Fortunately, there was an interest in the stories told by John Colter and other mountain men who had visited the Yellowstone. At first the stories were dismissed as preposterous tales without foundation, but they were repeated by reliable sources.

Abandoned beaver ponds, Grand Teton National Park.

The Creation of National Parks, Preserves, and Refuges

Help came for beavers at a critical time and in a most unusual way. In 1870, General Henry D. Washburn was Surveyor General of the Montana Territory. Nathaniel P. Langford and General Washburn gathered a small group to inspect the area and set the matter straight. They were joined by Lieutenant Gustavus Doane and a small group of infantry. The party was to become known as the Langford, Washburn, Doane Expedition. What they saw verified all the tales they had heard about the area. While at the last camp, the idea was put forth that the region was far too important to be divided into homesteads for private gain and that it should be set aside for permanent public use.

Cottonwoods and aspens were eaten by beavers or browsed off by elk many years ago. The only trees available are spruce and Lodgepole Pines. Grass and water lilies are the chief foods available to the beavers that live here.

In 1871, a geologist, Ferdinand V. Hayden, led an expedition that documented the unusual features of the area. After years of prodding and promotion by Langford, the idea finally caught on in the eastern United States. By an act of Congress on March 1, 1872, Yellowstone National Park was created. It was signed into law by President Ulysses S. Grant, and an area of 3472 square miles was closed to hunting and trapping. The few surviving beavers were given protection from trappers, and because there were no longer wolves or cougars in the park, the numbers of beavers increased rapidly.

Yellowstone National Park was created to protect a priceless scenic wonderland from private exploitation and to preserve it for the use and enjoyment of the public. Little did the politicians realize at the time the importance of their action. Yellowstone National Park was the first unit of the National Park System of the United States, and its creation set a precedent for not only the United States but for other nations around the world by which large areas were set aside and protected as national parks. Yellowstone also served as a model for the creation of state parks.

From the time this act of Congress was signed into law by President Grant, Yellowstone National Park became a 3472–square-mile wildlife refuge. This was a critical time for the elk as well as the beaver. It was the fashion of the time among well-dressed men to wear

After Yellowstone National Park was created by President Grant in 1872 beavers were the first animals to become firmly established in the new sanctuary. These old ponds were built by several generations of beavers over a period of years after the park was created. For a number of years they were the chief attraction for tourists there. Today beavers are rare in the park because the elk browse off every cottonwood seedling that takes root, leaving nothing for the beavers to eat.

an elk tusk as a decoration dangling from a watch chain. Each elk had two tusks, and they commanded high prices. As a result the animals were shot, the tusks knocked out, and the carcasses left to rot.

Poaching in the park became so flagrant that it was put under the protection of the United States Army, and it remained under army supervision until 1916 when it came under the jurisdiction of the Department of the Interior. Yellowstone National Park became a sanctuary at a critical time not only for the Beaver and the Elk, but also the Grizzly Bear, the Moose, and Trumpeter Swan when their numbers were at an all time low. A small surviving herd of wild buffalo was also driven into the park and granted protection.

From the time that the Yellowstone area was set aside as a national park, it has attracted visitors from across the country and around the world. No place on earth can begin to match it for its concentration of scenic wonders. However, from the beginning, observing wildlife in the park has been one of the greatest visitor activities. In earlier days, watching beavers at work and feeding the grizzlies were two of its greatest attractions. Yellowstone National Park played a key role in getting the public interested in preserving our wildlife heritage.

The Beaver, the Bison, Grizzly Bear, Pronghorn Antelope, Mountain Goat, Bighorn Sheep, Elk, Trumpeter Swan, and Whooping Crane were eventually saved as a result of this movement. However, the wisest of laws protecting wildlife and their most rigid enforcement were not enough to protect many endangered species, and the Passenger Pigeon, Heath Hen, Carolina Parakeet, and Labrador Duck were lost. What was most needed was large tracts of suitable habitat.

The creation of Yellowstone National Park was a giant step in the right direction. The results were both direct and indirect. First, as a large sanctuary for wildlife it set an example that was followed across the country and around the world. More help came on July 4, 1901, when President William McKinley set aside 59,020 acres of former Indian Reservation in Oklahoma as the Wichita Mountains Forest Preserve. His purpose was to have it used as a place where plains-dwelling settlers could come to get wood.

In summer, the beaver follows the flowing water up the sides of the mountains and builds terraces and dams well up into the Alpine Meadows which are home to Bighorn Sheep and Mountain Goats like these and the Hoary Marmot.

In 1905, William T. Hornaday and a number of others who were concerned with the future of the buffalo organized the American Bison Society. They demanded that the buffalo be given care and protection. Hornaday, at the time, was also director of the New York Zoological Society. The society offered to donate fifteen animals to the Government if Congress would appropriate sufficient funds to fence an area in the Wichita Mountains National Forest where they could be released. President Theodore Roosevelt persuaded Congress to appropriate $15,000 to build a fence around 8000 acres. On June 2, 1905, by Presidential Proclamation, he declared the National Forest as a National Wildlife Refuge, the first such unit in the United States. On October 11, 1907, fifteen of the finest buffaloes from the New York Zoological Society were shipped by rail to Oklahoma, and seven days later the six bulls and nine cows were safely returned to the plains and mountains. Later the refuge became a haven for the last of the Texas Longhorn cattle.

None of the National Wildlife Refuges was created to protect the beaver, but on many, beavers have returned and become firmly established. This includes a few that now live within the 59,020 acres of

Once nearly extinct, the buffalo is now being given protection in a number of wildlife refuges, like this pair. Long ago, wherever there were cottonwood trees along the flowing streams, the beaver shared grasslands with the buffalo.

Moose, Canada Geese, Trumpeter Swans and ducks take full advantage of the old beaver ponds in Yellowstone, Grand Teton, and Canadian National Parks.

the Wichita Mountains Wildlife Refuge that they share with the Bison, Longhorn Cattle, Elk, Wild Turkey, Prairie Dogs, and waterfowl.

In 1830, there were few areas east of the Mississippi River where the beaver and many other forms of displaced wildlife could survive, even if given rigid protection. This was a condition that man had created, but in doing so, he was oblivious to the consequences of his activities.

By the time the first settlers began to move inland, the beaver had been exterminated or was a very rare animal in the places where it had managed to survive. With settlement, the environment was rapidly changed to the degree that if the beaver did return, there were few places where it could survive. Most of eastern North America was once covered with climax forests of primarily hardwoods, and among them were stands of magnificent trees centuries old.

The settlers regarded the forest as an enemy to be conquered. To them, it represented a source of danger as a hiding place for Indians who might raid their villages and farms, and it sheltered "varmints" that preyed upon poultry, killed livestock, and ate crops. At best, the trees "were just standing there."

97

First, large areas of submarginal land were cleared for farming that should have been left to grow timber. The forests rapidly disappeared as people cut down trees for fuel and to for building ships, buildings, and furniture, while many others were turned into charcoal or cut down and burned simply to clear the land.

Newly cleared land at first produced bountiful crops, but as a result of poor agricultural practices, the soil became thinner and the crop yields progressively poorer. He plowed up and down the hillsides and made no attempt to save the topsoil. As a result, every time it rained and during the spring runoff of melting snow, topsoil that took

This small beaver pond is located in abandoned farm country, notice the old apple orchard in the background to the left. The site was probably chosen the previous year because no resident beavers occupied the area. However a beaver family could not live long here because of the scarcity of trees. Note the splash made by the resident beaver in the center right of the pond.

centuries to make, ran off the hillsides into the streams and down the rivers.

He pastured cattle along the water courses, and the hooves of the animals broke down the banks and turned streams into open ditches. In the absence of trees and brush, their flows ranged from trickle to torrent, depending upon the volume of runoff.

During the second decade of the twentieth century, after World War I and during the years of the Depression that followed, small farms no longer supported the families that owned them. One by one they were abandoned, and there was an exodus of farm families to places where wage work was available and industry provided a far better standard of living than farming.

Fortunately, worn-out land will grow cellulose, and nature moved in to reclaim it, first with grasses, then with brambles, and finally young trees were also beginning to grow in the areas where the timber had been cut by lumbermen and where settlers had indiscriminately cleared the land for farms. As a result, conditions along the stream valleys rapidly began to improve. Whitetail Deer and other forms of wildlife that had not been seen there for over a century gradually began to return.

As a result, hunters, fishermen, and others interested in the outdoors organized conservation clubs that were both social and political. They lobbied legislatures and the United States Congress, and eventually abandoned farms that had been taken over for unpaid taxes or purchased for a few dollars an acre were combined into hunting camps, game management areas, wildlife sanctuaries, and parks.

The Birth of the Conservation Movement

A strong conservation movement gradually gained momentum in the early days of the twentieth century. This was brought about because of a growing sentiment against the slaughter of wildlife by market hunters and the unrestricted killing of birds by plume hunters to supply birds and feathers to the millinery trade to decorate women's hats. Many species were brought to the verge of extinction. Several organizations were formed to stop the killing and to give special protection to threatened species. Some of the actions were direct. Breeding areas were purchased and protected by wardens. Conservationists lobbied legislatures and had laws passed and enforced that made it illegal to take, possess, buy, sell, or wear certain types of feathers. Enforcement was not always easy, and unknown numbers of wardens were killed by poachers.

Protection of wildlife was necessary, and it came at a crucial time, but protection was not enough. There was also the critical need to

Mule Deer with antlers in velvet in the vicinity of Banff Park, Canada in July.

acquire and protect large areas of suitable habitat. Conservation-minded sportsmen organized into local and regional conservation clubs that were both social and political, and as a result of their efforts, legislation was passed that provided funds for public lands and restoration of habitat. It was done through license fees, fines collected from violators, duck stamps paid for by hunters of migrating wildfowl, and especially through Pittman Robertson funds from taxes on firearms and ammunition. These go for the acquisition and support of wildlife refuges.

Most of the early wildlife conservation efforts were directed toward improving the conditions for hunting and fishing. Native species were protected during breeding seasons. Exotic species like the Ringneck Pheasant were imported and released, and there were game farms where other birds and animals were bred and released. One of the greatest successes was the restoration of the Whitetail Deer. It was accomplished by abolishing hunting with dogs and killing does. Man had also eliminated, in most areas, cougars and wolves, and as a result, there are probably more deer in eastern North America than ever before. In fact, in some agricultural areas the deer has come into conflict with man's interests.

The deer population spread without man's help, but the beaver had been either exterminated in many parts of its former range or it existed in such small numbers and was so widely dispersed that it was difficult for them to find mates. In 1901, there was only one wild beaver known to be living in New York State in Tupper Lake. The 1902 Annual Report of the Pennsylvania Game Commission by Dr. Joseph Kalbfus reads, "We are reliably informed that there is still a colony of beaver in this state, they are found in the wildest portion of a wild section."

In the early decades of the twentieth century, there was a growing desire among organized sportsmen to restore forms of wildlife that had existed before the days of intensive settlement. They especially wished to bring back the beaver as a valuable fur-bearing resource. Little did they realize at the time the impact that the restoration of the beaver to its former habitat would have on wildlife and the environment.

Beaver Restoration in the Northeastern United States

In 1904, New York State imported and released four beavers taken from Yellowstone National Park into the Adirondacks. Later, when Lake Superior-strain animals from Michigan were available, a quiet campaign was conducted by the Bureau of Game of the New York State Department of Conservation to eliminate the "yellow" beavers. As a result, all the beavers in northern New York are descendents of Lake Superior stock. Those in the Southern Tier counties are descendents of animals that crossed over the state line from Pennsylvania.

The trap-and-transfer method of moving beavers to resettle them in new areas proved to be highly successful. The first problem was to capture them uninjured. Leg-gripping traps were not the answer even when the jaws of the trap were padded. Vernon Bailey solved the problem by inventing the Bailey beaver trap, a cage trap that captures the animals uninjured. They can even be transported short distances without removal from the trap.

Restoration programs were likewise successful in Pennsylvania. In the summer of 1917, a pair of beavers from Wisconsin were released in East Crowley Run, Cameron County. They reproduced rapidly, and over the next three years, twenty-eight additional pairs were liberated in various game refuges. A short eleven years later, there were fifteen hundred known colonies in forty-nine Pennsylvania counties.

The first trapping season in Pennsylvania was in 1934, and 6400 beavers were taken. Little did the members of the Pennsylvania Game Commission realize at its inception the far-reaching results of the game restoration that they had initiated. It was to serve as a guide that was followed in many other places. Moreover, wildlife does not recognize

101

Picture of young Black Bear taken in Allegany State Park on the New York-Pennsylvania border. The Black Bear was extinct by 1850 in most eastern farm areas. Today the Black Bear makes full use of the edge conditions created by the beavers.

political boundaries. First the Whitetail Deer, then the Beaver, and later, the Black Bear and the Wild Turkey wandered across the border and restocked New York State's Southern Tier counties from which they moved north into western and central New York and into the Catskills. Wildlife from Pennsylvania also moved east into New Jersey, south into Delaware and Maryland, and west into Ohio.

Beaver Restoration in Canada

In the most remote areas of Maine and eastern Canada, a few beavers had managed to survive. With man's help and protection and the absence of predators like wolves and cougars, there was a dramatic increase in the beaver population. Wherever suitable habitat could be found, the animals rapidly spread westward. In the meantime, beavers were moving down from the high Rockies and spreading east.

Probably the greatest and certainly the most widely publicized trap-and-transfer program to restore the beaver to its former range was the one carried out in the James Bay drainage system of Canada. From a small start it gained momentum until it involved the governments of

Swampy Cree guide with Blue Geese at the Hannah Bay hunting camp on James Bay.

Quebec, Ontario, the Indian Affairs Branch at Ottawa, Hudson's Bay Company, the Anglican and Roman Catholic Churches, and many interested individuals, especially the Swampy Crees who live around the bay.

James Bay is that long arm of Hudson's Bay that thrusts deep down into Canada. It is surrounded by vast areas of muskeg that has been one of the prime breeding areas for ducks, geese, and Tundra Swans. It also is the area from which many thousands of beaver skins have been taken by the Crees who brought them to the trading posts. From there they were collected and shipped to London.

Years of overtrapping by the Crees around James Bay had so reduced the beaver population that every year families had to travel farther and farther inland to find places where beavers still lived. Every year the number of skins brought in to the trading posts decreased. As the beavers disappeared, so did the ponds that they built and maintained with the result that other forms of wildlife that had depended on them for sources of food and places to live also became reduced in numbers. There were fewer water lilies, an important source of food for moose, and the scarcity of fish and frogs resulted in a reduction in the mink population. The ponds that had been used by waterfowl were gone, resulting in a drastic decrease in the numbers of geese and ducks. The Crees, who depended upon hunting and fishing as sources of livelihood, were in desperate straits.

In the season of 1928–1929, only four beaver pelts were brought to the Hudson's Bay Post at Rupert House. The manager of the post at the time was a Scot named James Watt. He was deeply concerned about the situation, especially the plight of the Crees who were destitute, on relief, and in debt to the Company.

In 1930, an Indian came to James Watt and told him that he had discovered two active beaver houses and asked for credit to get supplies for an expedition to get the beavers that lived in them. James Watt's answer was, "I will buy the *cabain*. Those are my beavers. Do not kill them." He paid for them out of his own pocket.

James Watt was not able to leave the post, but his wife, Maude Watt, went to see L. A. Richard, Deputy Minister of Game and Fisheries of Quebec. He was interested in the possibilities of the plan, and she returned with a lease of 7200 square miles of territory between the Rupert and Eastmain Rivers to be used as a beaver preserve.

The next step was to get the cooperation of the Indians. He called together a council of the band of Crees who hunted the wilderness around Rupert House. They in turn, called in their people from the forests and rivers for a tribal get-together to discuss the beaver situation. On the basis of survival of two young per family each year, he demonstrated the expected population increase by using matches. Later he made charts that were published by Hudson's Bay Company that showed the expected increase over a ten-year period. The table was translated into Cree syllabic by Fred McLeod, the Post Manager at Oskelaneo.

Both federal and provincial governments became interested and took an active part in what was going on. They sent their own personnel to Rupert House and established headquarters there. Twenty Indian leaders were appointed "beaver watchers," and each was to receive a stipend of $100.00 per year plus a windbreaker and a badge.

In 1930, there were only 25 known beavers in the preserve. The first official count was made in 1933, and the numbers had increased to 162 working beavers. Every year the "beaver watchers" made a count. To avoid duplication, each house was given a distinctive marking. Five years later, the population increased to 3300 and the following year to 4000. In 1940, the preserve was opened to trapping. From that time until 1948, over 13,000 skins were harvested. On the basis of continued limited trapping, the beaver population within this preserve has stabilized to between 13,000 and 15,000 or about two beavers per square mile.

The Watts had powerful friends in high government positions who became involved in the program to restore the beaver population to the James Bay Region. Three who were probably closest to them were L. A. Richard, Deputy Minister of Fur Services, Quebec; J. A. Trembly, Director of Fur Services, Quebec; and Hugh R. Conn, General Supervisor of Wildlife and Fisheries, Ottawa.

The Crees played a crucial role in the rapid distribution of the beaver population. Each family had its ancestral territory and wished to stock it with as many beavers as fast as possible. Natural increase and spread of population alone could never have distributed so many beavers over so wide a territory in so short a time.

The efforts of James and Maude Watt to restore the beaver was a story of great human interest and the news media took full advantage of the opportunity, with the result that their work received wide public support, which played a major role in its success. Newspapers across Canada and the United States regularly reported on its progress. Magazines, including *The Saturday Evening Post*, featured stories about it, and listeners heard about it on radio. In the motion picture theaters, audiences saw newsreel films of Swampy Cree Indians receiving beavers and transporting them across vast areas of muskeg to the places where they were released.

The success on the east coast led to the establishment of similar sanctuaries elsewhere. Conditions on the west coast had been as bleak as those on the east, and there was only one known occupied beaver house in the Attawapiskat region north of the Kapisko River. With the cooperation of the Northwest Territories Administration in 1934, Charlton Island became a beaver preserve. The next year Agameski Island was also made a preserve. From the beaver populations of these two islands beavers were captured and relocated on the mainland. In 1938, the Indian Affairs Branch at Ottawa took up the idea and created beaver preserves on James Bay.

In 1940, the Ontario Government set up a three-thousand-square-mile preserve at Albany on the west coast. Beavers were taken from Charlton and Agamenski Islands for restocking. That was before timber wolves had moved into Algonquin Park in southern Ontario. The beaver population there was at its peak and a large number were live-trapped there and transported north for restocking around James Bay.

The Rupert House Preserve lies between the Rupert River on the south and Eastmain River on the north, and it extends from James Bay deep into Quebec on the east. This was the first area set aside as a beaver preserve, but others were created in rapid succession and in each, the lessons learned at Rupert House were put into effect. Within a few years, contiguous wildlife preserves bordered the entire shore lines on both sides and on the south of James Bay. The shore line is many hundreds of miles in length, and each preserve extends inland from the bay from one hundred to several hundred miles. When this system was completed, Rupert House Preserve was one of the smaller units. Some of the preserves are administered by Hudson's Bay Company, the remainder by the Indian Affairs branch of the Dominion Government.

The rapidly increasing numbers of beavers and the new ponds they created and maintained brought improved conditions for fish, amphibians, breeding waterfowl, and many other forms of wildlife.

The greatest change brought about by the return of the beaver was in the lives of the Swampy Cree Indians who live around the bay. In 1930, when they assembled at Rupert House to hear James Watt reveal his plan to restore the beaver population, they were starving and deeply in debt. They agreed first to a ban on trapping beavers for five years and later extended it to ten. At the end of that period, with the dramatic increase in the numbers of beavers, the Crees became prosperous for the first time in their lives. Instead of being in debt to the trading posts, they were building up credits, and instead of several families sharing a canoe, each one had its own as well as an outboard motor to propel it.

Many of the Swampy Crees today live very much in the manner of their ancestors. A large part of the food they eat comes from the fish they net and the birds and animals they shoot and trap. The Cree women are very skillful in tanning and making things to wear from leather, especially moosehide, but the things they must buy at the trading posts must be paid for chiefly with furs. The most important of these is the fur of the beaver.

Today the mainstay of the Cree population living in this region of northern Canada is a thriving beaver population. It is a carefully managed resource. Overpopulation would severely deplete their food supply and result in starvation. On the other hand, unrestricted trapping would invite the return of conditions as they were in 1928–1929 when four beaver skins were brought into the trading post at Rupert House. Then the beaver was threatened with extinction and the Crees with starvation. Today, trapping is done on a sustained yield basis. In each district is a government-employed beaver warden who patrols the area assigned to him and determines how many beaver skins each family can take from its ancestral territory during a trapping season without danger of reducing the population for the next season.

Algonquin guide demonstrating the use of the tump line in carrying awkward shaped and heavy objects across portages. The tump line is a long piece of leather, wide in the middle and tapering toward both ends, which are tied around the object to be carried. The wide part goes across the forehed and requires powerful neck and shoulder muscles.

Exact official titles may vary but to the Crees, any person in charge of any operation is referred to as "the boss." Therefore, to the Crees, the warden becomes "The Beaver Boss."

At Rupert House is a little pile of stones on which there is an inscription that reads, "Here in September 1668 Captain Gilham and Choudard des Groseilliers landed, spent the winter and built a cabin which they called 'Fort Charles.'" The following spring they sailed home with a ship loaded with beaver skins. The landing of *The Nonesuch* was the beginning of a series of events that determined the course of history in North America. History was changed again from this very spot when Post Manager James Watt called his meeting with the Crees in 1930 to initiate the program which has restored the beaver to Rupert's Land.

107

The Spruce Grouse prefers to live among the conifers of the northern states and eastern Canada and can be found around the beaver ponds there. However, its southern range overlaps that of the Ruffed Grouse which is chiefly a bird of the hardwoods.

A number of years ago, when I was working on the documentary film, *Land of the Blue Goose,* it was my extreme good fortune to be aboard the Hudson's Bay Company ship, *The Fort Charles,* on its roundup trip for the season. On that trip I had excellent opportunities to observe and film many aspects of the lives of the Swampy Crees that live along the east coast of James Bay. One port of call was an overnight stay at Rupert House. On that trip, the chief deck cargo consisted of canoes made in New Brunswick. They were most convincing visual evidence that the economic condition of the Crees had improved dramatically. For many years canoes had been made at Rupert House but apparently some of the Crees not only preferred the imports but were prepared to pay for them.

The range of the beaver once covered a large part of Alaska, Canada, the lower forty-eight states of the United States, and extended well down into Mexico. Because of unrestricted trapping, it became a very rare animal, threatened with extinction, but with man's help, it returned to many parts of its former range, not only in Canada and Mexico but also in every state of the Union except Hawaii. The beaver has again become a most valuable fur-bearer. However, the value of the monetary return from the sale of beaver skins is heavily outweighed by his ability to create ideal living conditions for many other forms of wildlife.

4

Beaver Works

It is difficult to consider that any creature could have occupied an area so vast, under conditions so varied, in the presence of such large enemies; yet the beaver's range and former numbers attest to the fact that it was highly successful in adapting to a wide range of types of terrain, temperature, climate, and predators.

Nature was in a generous mood when she endowed him. She gave to the beaver two special advantages for survival. One is the ability to eat and digest any form of plant life that is available to him, and that includes some forms that are poisonous to many other creatures. The other is the unusual ability to change his environment to suit the special needs of himself and his family.

Beavers are famous for their ability to build dams and store water, but there are places where some of them have lived out their lives without ever building a dam or living in a house. Those living this way are known as bank beavers. They once lived in dens dug in to the sides of cliffs along the Missouri, the Mississippi, and every other large river and along most of the lakes in North America.

Most rivers are subject to alternating periods of low water and floods, and for this reason dens are often dug out above high-water level. Today beavers are again living in holes dug into the banks of the Rio Grande where it flows past Big Bend National Park in Texas. Summer visitors to Zion National Park in Utah may see the Virgin River as a placid stream and are perhaps thus puzzled when they see beaver dens dug into the stream bank several feet above the water. This stream may be placid when the visitors see it, but there are times when it becomes a raging torrent.

Water is absolutely necessary for the beaver's survival. It must be deep enough so he is never locked in or frozen out of his house by ice for he and his family must be able to travel under the ice to and from the food pile that they stored for winter. Water provides safety from enemies, and it also makes it easy for the beaver family to transport building materials and to store a food supply.

109

A beaver pond on a frosty November morning just before the pond froze over. Notice the large house and well stocked foodpile in the background and the straight, high, beaver-made dam in the foreground.

Dams

Where Nature has not provided water deep enough to suit his needs, the beaver builds dams and maintains ponds. When one first views a large beaver dam and considers the amount of material it contains, it is difficult to believe that this was done by beavers and was not the work of human hands. We are prone to think of these accomplishments in human terms. Therefore, it is natural to conclude, as early European explorers did, that a dam of this size is the result of many beavers working together, even to the degree that it was constructed according to a preconceived plan and under the direction of a boss beaver.

A large beaver dam is rather the result of a family of beavers working together over a period of time, and in some circumstances, where a pond has been abandoned and reoccupied a number of times, the dam represents the contributions of the work of several generations of beavers. At any time, however, the maximum number of beavers working on a dam probably does not exceed six—two adults with some assistance from four subadults. However, that does not rule out the possibility that later in the season, some of the kits might make some contributions also.

Work seldom stops with the building of a single dam. As soon as work on the main dam is well underway, at least one secondary dam is

110

built a short distance downstream. This is a very sound engineering practice, for it relieves pressure on the main dam and reduces water loss from the pond through seepage. It is the usual practice to build a number of other secondary dams downstream as well as another series of dams upstream, and when a family of beavers lives in an area for a number of years, it is not unusual for three quarters of a mile or more to be terraced with dams, ponds, and water impoundments.

A secondary dam may sometimes be enlarged to the extent that it becomes the main dam, thereby considerably increasing the area of the pond behind it. Water backed up behind the series of dams makes it possible for members of the family to move with ease and safety up and down the stream. As they travel, they often pause to eat, and this they can do without leaving the water or traveling far from it. This relieves pressure on the available food supply in the immediate vicinity of the pond. The ponds and smaller water impoundments upstream can be critical to survival during dry periods. Without the water stored in them, the streams might cease to flow, causing the ponds to dry up and forcing the beavers to move.

A family of beavers over a period of time will move an amazing quantity of material in building a dam, but it has a humble beginning. It is started by an individual or a pair, and the site selected is typically a place where the stream banks are relatively high and close together. It is begun with fresh-cut brush dragged downstream and piled across the current with the butt ends pressed into or against the banks. More brush is piled on it in the same manner, and then it is weighted down with stones or pieces of sod broken off the banks. As the force of the current pushes against it, the mass becomes firmly wedged into the banks.

The next step is to plaster mud against the upstream side of the dam to make it watertight. The process is repeated until the dam reaches the tops of the banks. When water begins to flow around the ends, wings are added, and the dam grows longer.

The shape that a dam will assume depends upon its location. It follows the contours of the land. When water flows over the top of the break, it is stopped with freshly cut brush and mud, and likewise, when water begins to flow around the ends, the dam is lengthened with new material. Freshly cut poles, some peeled, some not, are dragged over the top of the dam and laid on the downstream side.

Anything that can be pushed, pulled, carried, dragged, or floated goes into the dam. When a stick or pole has been stripped of its bark, it is either carried up and laid on the top of the house or dragged over the top of the dam and placed on the downstream side. Rocks the size of a person's head are commonly found in a dam, especially in its early stages, and there is the one that Enos Mills (13) mentioned that

111

This is the downstream side of a newly started beaver dam. Note the number of stones used in the dam. Anything that can be pushed, pulled, carried, dragged, or floated goes into the dam; even some very heavy objects are used. As the dam grows older and is built higher the stones will not show, they will be covered by layers of sticks, poles and dirt dragged out of the pond and over the dam.

weighed one hundred twenty pounds. All manner of trash and junk that man throws away goes into the dams: tires, oil drums, beverage cans, and even traps with their chains and the stakes that held them have been found in beaver dams. As a result, the bottom of a beaver pond is cleaner than that of a natural or a man-made pond.

The beaver's ability to move heavy objects has long been well known, but whether these things were accomplished by individuals working alone or through cooperation has been difficult to determine. The beaver's work habits have not made it easy to observe him in action. In many places, most of his work is done at night, and there are many situations where beavers avoid the presence of man. There is, however, at least one authenticated report that confirms the fact that beavers will cooperate on moving heavy objects. Dorothy Richards (15) maintained a beaver sanctuary near Doldgeville, New York. For a number of years she observed a pair of beavers, Sampson and Delilah. and wrote about them in her book, *Beaversprite.*

This is the upstream side of a recently drained beaver dam showing the mud which is plastered on the dam to keep it watertight and the trench from which the mud was dug to plaster the dam. Trappers killed the beavers that had been living here, a month earlier.

This is the same dam as pictured on the previous page; note that the stones can no longer be seen. This is a secondary dam, downstream from the main dam in a place unsuited to make a large pond, but will facilitate travel and relieve pressure on the main dam.

113

The beavers worked separately as a rule, but whenever cooperation was needed they worked as a team. One day I saw Sampson and Lila get together to move a heavy log. They fastened their teeth in the log at strategic locations and with their feet firmly anchored on the ground they shoved mightily. They moved the log some distance and then let go with their teeth and rested for a few minutes. After a bit, as though through a signal, they tackled the job again.

Another fascinating aspect of beaver behavior has been revealed by Peter W. Hanney (10) in *Rodents and Their Habits.* He reports that dam building is an instinctive reaction rather than a learned process and that orphan beavers with no experience and that had never seen one can be stimulated to action and start building a dam. The stimulus is the sound of water running over stones, and work continues as long as the sound can be heard. He also found that the tape-recorded sounds of running water were as effective as the actual sounds of running water.

When a pair of beavers moves into and occupies a new territory, a favorite location is in the middle of a stand of trees. The dam they build is usually started at some time during the summer, and work progresses at an increasingly rapid rate until ice begins to form. It is usually of modest size, but it must hold back enough water so they can travel freely under the ice.

If they have been fortunate enough to find a location in the middle of a stand of trees, the first year is the easiest. They can gather their winter food supply without making long trips over land with the ever-present danger from predators. That first winter they can dig up and eat live roots from the bottom of the pond, and they may live either in a house that they have started or in one of the dens that they might have dug into the banks shortly after they moved into the area.

The following spring there is a strong possibility that the size of the family will increase from two to six. Four kits is a common litter size. The larger family requires more food, and there is less in the immediate vicinity of the pond because the trees flooded by the water backed up behind the dam are dead. After the spring runoff the ice is off the pond, and work on the dam continues, with the greatest period of activity occurring when the leaves begin to change color in the fall.

During the second season, the dam is made longer, stronger, and possibly as much as a foot higher. Usually there is at least one and sometimes several secondary dams. The third season may see more height and length added to the dam and an increase in both the number and size of secondary dams. Thereafter, as long as a pond is occupied, work never stops on the dam. It will continue to be made thicker although seldom higher. The deepest part of the pond is

Dead conifers killed by flooding when beavers dammed the outlet and raised the lake level by at least four feet.

usually immediately above the dam because material has been dug up from the bottom to plaster the upstream side.

The average height of a dam is usually no more than six feet above the land, but there are exceptions. In some instances, in narrow, steep-sided valleys, there are dams in excess of fifteen feet high. The dam tends to be thickest in the middle and thinner at the ends. Thickness at the base of a dam may vary from less than eight to eighteen feet or more, and the width at the top from a few inches to over three feet, depending upon the time that beavers have been working on it.

Three favorite building materials are willow, osier, and alder. Unpeeled poles that have been dragged over the top of the dam and placed on the downstream side and pieces of brush that have been thrust into the top of the dam readily sprout and take root. As the roots grow, they lock the materials in the dam firmly in place. As a result, a beaver dam will withstand floods better than an earthen dam of the type that man makes. They spread out floodwaters, slow them down and reduce their capacity to do damage. As soon as the flood recedes, any breaks are soon repaired.

There are also times when floods add materials that the beavers would not be able to move to the dams. This is in the form of driftwood that often lodges lengthwise across the top of a dam and that may include large trees. When that happens, the beavers soon take advantage of the opportunity and incorporate this material in the dam, thereby making it stronger to resist future floods.

115

This dam in the Catskills of New York was built in a steep stream valley. It is approximately fifteen feet high and backed up a small but deep pond that was inhabited by some unusually large brook trout.

Enos Mills (13) mentioned a beaver dam that was 2140 feet long on the Jefferson River near Three Forks, Montana. More than half the dam was less than six feet in height, but there were two short sections that were twenty-three feet wide at the base, five feet wide on top, and fourteen feet high.

Morgan (14) described two types of beaver dams that he had observed in the Upper Peninsula of Michigan in the middle 1860s. One was the familiar stick dam, and the other was an earth-bank dam. This type is composed of solid earth with no stick work showing except at the overflow in the middle of the dam. These he concluded were dams that were started in the usual manner but were so old that all the wood that had been used in building them had long since decayed and disappeared. In every instance, the large mass of material in them represented the contributions of many generations of beavers. Each had been started many years and possibly centuries earlier. Only in a place where beavers have been in continuous residence could a dam of this type be observed.

Houses

The most familiar type of beaver home is the dome-shaped island house which stands in the middle of the pond, but the beavers that

116

Beaver pond built between two natural lakes in the vicinity of Tupper Lake, New York. Notice the house at the left in the background, built over the top of the bank borrow where the beavers first lived rather than in the center of the pond.

built it undoubtedly first lived in a den they dug into a stream bank when they first moved into the area. As long as they are in residence, they will dig numerous dens into the banks at strategic locations where they can rest or take refuge. In its territory, a beaver is seldom far from a den in which it can seek safety in time of emergency. The beaver was a digger of dens long before he became a builder of houses, and there are many beavers today that are living as bank beavers in places unsuited to the construction of ponds, especially along the banks of streams and rivers that are subject to floods.

Anyone fortunate enough to watch a beaver in action is impressed by the amount of material he can move in a short period of time. The claws on his front feet are very efficient digging tools. As fast as the earth is loosened, it is pushed back by the hind feet, and with a series of forward and backward movements, the loose material is cleared out of the tunnel. At the end there is a large chamber that can serve as living quarters.

A favorite place to dig a burrow is beneath the roots of a tree which will prevent the top from caving in. In many wooded areas of eastern Canada, New York, and New England, there are ponds and small lakes where, over the years, vegetation has advanced from the shore lines and covered considerable expanses of water with a thick

117

layer of sphagnum moss, pitcher plants, sundew, and other types of acid-bog plants. These expanses of floating vegetation are referred to as quaking bogs. Foot progress across one of them is like walking on a mattress.

Beavers inhabiting some of these bodies of water swim under rather than walk across them, and they cut holes in them where they wish to come out. They may also tunnel considerable distances inland before digging out above ground. The absence of dirt piles around these holes indicates that the digging was done from below.

Except for the trails leading out from them, it is often difficult to detect their presence, and it is surprising to find how far some of them are from open water. These holes make it easy for beavers to leave and return to the pond, and when pursued by an enemy, a beaver can dive into one of these holes and seek safety. For that reason, it may be appropriate to refer to them as plunge holes.

The regular type of house will be started soon after a pair of beavers has moved in and laid claim to an area. The site may be located at a favorite eating or resting place or near a flowing spring. In the beginning it is only a pile of brush or sticks with the center hollowed out, but once it is started, work proceeds rather rapidly. As poles are peeled of their bark, they are dragged to the top. Some of the poles, especially if they are alder, will be used unpeeled.

The house rapidly assumes the shape of a broad-based teepee. As water rises behind the dam, the ceiling of the room inside is cut away, and the material is trampled under foot. As the height of the water rises, the floor of the room must be raised accordingly, for at all times it must be several inches above water level. As the base of the structure widens, it begins to cover the places where the beavers leave and enter the water. The material that may interfere is cut away, and passageways from the room inside down to the bottom of the pond develop. There are at least two of these passages, and this is an excellent safety measure. If an enemy enters the house, the members of the family cannot be trapped inside because they have an escape route.

During the summer, the house is composed chiefly of sticks and poles, but as days grow shorter and nights get longer, it is plastered with mud, and when winter sets in, it is large enough to house a pair of beavers until spring arrives.

Another type of beaver lodge is the one that has been built at the side of the pond. When the beavers first move into an area and start building the dam, they live in a bank burrow. As the water level rises behind the dam, they dig away the top of the den until the roof caves in, and they then build a house over the top of the hole. Work proceeds on this type of house very much as it does on the island house.

The house built by a pair of beavers the first season will be large enough to comfortably house the pair that built it, but when kits are

Large regular beaver house in the center of a pond, showing a freshly peeled poplar pole, center, that was dragged up on the house during the previous night.

Cross section of a model beaver house built to represent the inside of a beaver house. A real house falls apart if one attempts to divide it. The model shows entrances on both the right and the left and the raised portion between, where the animals are above water.

119

Large beaver house, measuring thirty-two feet in length built on the side of Lake Massaweepie in a Boy Scout Camp in the Adirondacks near Gale, New York. The house was built in six feet of water.

born the following spring, it must be made larger. As the family grows still larger the following year and thereafter, the size must again be increased, and as long as a family occupies a house, it will continue to increase in size.

A house that has been occupied for a number of years must be large enough to provide space for a family of ten or even more: two adults, the subadults, and the kits. Each beaver lodge has distinctive individual characteristics, but there are some general rules that apply in their construction. The structure may stand six or seven feet above the bottom of the pond, and it may be fourteen or more feet in diameter at its base. The moat surrounding the house may be three feet wide and three or more feet in depth, and the height above water level is typically three to four feet. The chamber inside is dome-shaped, six or seven feet in diameter at the base and approximately two and one-half feet in height. The floor is hard-packed earth covered with finely shredded wood and only a few inches above water level when the pond is full.

The entrance tunnels must be wide enough to provide the beavers with sufficient room to bring in sticks from their wood pile and are usually about fifteen inches in diameter. The side walls are from two to three feet thick in the average house.

One special feature of the house that often goes unnoticed is the "chimney" which lets stale air out and fresh air in. Without it, the family

120

An empty beaver house shown after spring freshets breached the dam. Trappers had killed the resident beavers about a month earlier. This large house had three tunnels for entering and exiting. The main entrance is shown in front. The length of poplar log in front was cut and thrown into the pond by a man the preceding September.

A beaver house snug and secure from predators in the frozen pond in February.

121

The summer after trappers killed the beavers in France Brook the stream went dry. The following year a pair of beavers moved to the headwaters, repaired the dam, and reoccupied and repaired the house. Notice the long, low, rambling dam of this pond.

of beavers living inside would soon exhaust their supply of fresh air. This vent is only a thin spot in the roof that has not been plastered over. On a cold winter day a thin whisp of steam may be seen rising above the top of the house, evidence that the house is occupied by a family of beavers.

As long as a lodge is occupied, new material is added to it. As a result, some become very large. One on the side of Lake Massaweepie near Tupper Lake, New York, was twenty-six feet in diameter at the surface of the lake, the top was at least four and a half feet above water, and the structure stood in at least four feet of water. It was not possible to measure the total diameter at the bottom of the lake. Because of the rocky terrain, this house was constructed chiefly of poles and billets of wood. Wherever beavers live, be it in a den dug into a bank or inside a house, their living quarters are a few inches above water, reasonably dry, clean, and carpeted with finely shredded wood.

Ponds

Every beaver pond has its own distinctive characteristics. To a large degree, its ultimate size, shape, and depth depend upon the site selected for the dam and the manner in which it is built. A short dam

The flooded area in an old beaver meadow after the old original dam has been repaired by a new pair of beavers. Note the Spatterdock or Yellow Water Lilies growing in the pool below the dam because this dam has been backed up by a secondary one downstream. This pond is on a game management area of the New York State Dept. of Environmental Conservation.

built in a strategic location may back up water to create a pond that is deep and covers a large area. On the other hand, a low rambling dam may result in a pond that is small and shallow. Ponds may vary from a fraction of an acre to over fifty acres in area.

Where dams are built in steep-sided valleys, they may form ponds that are twelve or fifteen feet deep, but the average pond is seldom more than four feet deep except immediately above the dam and around the base of the house. In shallower ponds that may be covered with thick layers of ice for long periods of time, beavers often dig out channels in the pond bottoms along the routes they must travel during the winter. One condition that is absolutely necessary for the survival of a beaver family is a pond that is deep enough so that ice can never freeze deep enough to lock them into or out of their living quarters. On rare occasions this has been known to happen with beavers but with far greater frequency with muskrats.

Even in places where man or nature has provided bodies of water for them, beavers are seldom satisfied with conditions as they find them. Wherever they come upon water that is flowing, they cannot seem to resist the urge to dam it. The National Audubon Society maintains a nature center in Sharon, Connecticut, and on it is a rather large, man-made lake. Beavers moved in and built a dam across the top of a masonry dam and thereby added considerably to the height of the water and the area covered by the lake. Raquette Lake is one of the larger bodies of water in the Adirondack Mountains of New York State. Beavers found water flowing from its outlet, built a dam across it, and raised the water level by over two feet. Behavior of this type among beavers is the rule rather than the exception.

In places that do not favor the building of a large pond, it is common practice for a family of beavers to build and maintain more than one pond. One family that lived along a small stream known as France Brook in Allegany State Park near Salamanca, New York, first lived in a house standing in the middle of a small pond. They extended their activities upstream for over half a mile. During that time they built and maintained twelve dams of various sizes which held back bodies of water that terraced the valley. Two of them were ponds as large as the original pond. Except for trips over the tops of the dams, the members of this family could travel freely up and down the stream for three-quarters of a mile. In the middle pond they built a second house, occupied it one winter, and then moved back into the original house.

From the time that water first begins to back up behind a dam and as long as a pond is in existence, a beaver pond undergoes constant change. This is most dramatic where the pond is created in a heavily wooded area. In many instances backed-up water kills a far greater number of trees than what is cut for food and for building material for as long as the pond is occupied. A new pond of this type will at first be cluttered with standing dead timber, but over the years a combination of forces, including high winds, moving ice, high water, the activities of the beavers, and decay, will eliminate most of this dead material, and the life forms in the area impounded will rapidly change from terrestrial to aquatic. When a pond has been occupied and active over a period of years, it usually supports the growth of water plants, including water lilies, even in the most unlikely locations. Particularly common are the Yellow Pond Lily or Spatterdock.

All beaver ponds have one feature in common: each one is temporary. There are numerous instances in which a beaver family that has occupied and maintained a pond for years will suddenly decide to move, abandon the pond en masse, and start another in a new location. In these cases, the move is probably made because the supply of food trees within convenient traveling distance from the pond has been exhausted. There are also occasions where ponds fill with silt, but the most frequent cause of an abandoned pond is the trapper.

A beaver dam requires constant maintenance, and when there are no beavers to keep it in repair, breaks develop in it and the water

A few years before this picture was taken this was a prime hunting area for Ruffed Grouse, deer, Cottontail Rabbits, and Grey Squirrels. Beavers flooded the area and turned it into a breeding area for waterfowl and an excellent place to fish for Bullheads and Large-mouth Black Bass. This pond is on game management land near Canton, New York.

escapes. A drained pond becomes a mud flat. This, however, is a temporary condition, for a freshly drained pond makes an ideal seed bed, and within a very short time, seeds that have lain dormant in the mud and those that are carried in by wind, birds, or animals, soon sprout, take root, and turn the pond bottom into a beaver meadow with a lush growth of grasses and forbs. The most rapid regeneration of vegetation is usually along the top of the dam. The living twigs that the beavers thrust into it grow rapidly and form a dense hedge which clearly marks the location of a former beaver dam.

In the meantime, in the area that was cleared around the pond, there is sprout growth from stumps and roots of trees cut by beavers in addition to the growth of new seedlings. Within a few years the area is covered with a dense growth of bushes, brambles, and shrubs. These, in turn, are eventually overtopped by saplings.

When a new growth of saplings becomes established around a former beaver pond, the situation is ideal for a pair of beavers to move in and reoccupy it. In many instances they only need to repair a break

125

A recently abandoned beaver pond at France Brook. The dam has been breached and the pond is nearly empty, creating a mud flat. Note the sticks in the background left scattered in the mud of the pond bottom by the beavers.

Muskrat house in a beaver pond which appears to have been built on the top of a ridge that is the remnant of an old beaver dam. The picture was taken at the headwaters of France Brook a year after it was reoccupied.

in the old dam. Just as often, however, they build a new one, and it is not unusual to see the remains of an old dam in the middle of a new pond.

Wherever beavers have been left undisturbed by man, ponds have been built, occupied, abandoned, and later reoccupied for centuries. Their works have created clearings in stands of climax forests, and entire stream valleys have been terraced with dams, ponds, and beaver meadows. In this type of situation, every pond and clearing becomes an oasis for creatures of the forest in a wildlife desert of green.

Food Piles

In many areas the price of survival for the beaver is his ability to dam water deep enough so that he can travel freely under the ice during the long winter months. In those places it is of equal importance that in times of plenty, he and his family build up a food supply that will sustain them until they can break out from under the ice to get fresh food. There are times for weeks on end when bark from their food pile may be their sole source of sustenance. Beavers are not the only creatures that store food, but no other form of wildlife stores it in such quantities or depends upon it so heavily for survival. Comparison of weights of young beavers in the fall and again in the spring indicate that very little growth takes place during the winter months.

The quantity of food that beavers store varies according to location. Those living where winters are long and severe must store it in large quantities. On the other hand, Kenneth C. Smith (17), in *Beaver in Louisiana*, stated that in that area food is available at all times during the year, and therefore beavers do not store food as they must do farther north.

The building of the food pile starts when days begin to grow shorter, often early in September. Freshly cut brush is dragged to the main entrance of the house or burrow. In the past, it was sometimes claimed that the beavers sucked the air out of the wood to make it sink, but actually it is full of sap, and it easily becomes waterlogged. Also every day new material is dragged to the top of the pile. Layer upon layer of new material is added, and the weight of the accumulated material presses the lower layers firmly into the mud in the bottom of the pond. The materials in the pile are chiefly brush, but there will also be poles and sections of small logs six to eight inches in diameter. This work goes on at an increasingly rapid pace until ice forms on the pond. Then, all work stops.

Whenever a member of the beaver family is hungry, it needs only to go outside, cut a stick from the food pile, bring it in, peel it, and eat the bark from it. After that has been done, the peeled stick is dragged out, and it sinks to the bottom of the pond. When spring arrives, these discarded sticks are picked up and dragged over the top of the dam. Two early spring activities are making repairs to the dam and cleaning the pond of the peeled sticks that were dragged out of the house during the winter.

Trails

Many forms of wildlife are prone to follow precisely the same routes in their daily travels. As a result these sometimes develop into beaten game trails that are heavily used. In the case of the beaver, the trails are used not only for travel but to transport food and building material as well. Some are as straight as if the course had been laid out with a transit. In each instance, on its first trip, the beaver literally follows its nose to a distant stand of food trees and follows the same route every time thereafter. These trails evolve from repeated use by a creature with eyesight that is poor and whose movements are directed

A heavily used trail being dug out to start a beaver canal. This leads to a source of water that will be diverted into the pond.

128

to a large extent by a sense of smell that is incredibly keen. Beavers often travel inland by one route and return to water by another, especially where the route followed back is down the side of a steep bank.

The paths that beavers make get much heavier use than ordinary game trails because of the repeated trips out on the land and back to the water for food and building materials. Anything that grows along the sides of these paths that may interfere with free passage of materials that are transported is cut away until these routes develop into well-traveled roadways with clearings on either side that grow wider because of demands for food and building materials. These clearings also provide a considerable measure of safety as they eliminate places where enemies may lurk undetected. The repeated dragging of brush down these roadways sweeps them clean, and the heavier material that is dragged down to the water wears down the center paths. From these roadways side trails may branch off, often to join another trail. In places where beavers regularly travel and transport materials down the sides of steep banks, they take full advantage of gravity, and with heavy use they resemble the chutes that loggers use to skid logs down steep hillsides. These become the U-shaped beaver slides of the types that early travelers up the Missouri River described. They make it easy for the beavers to get their cuttings to water and also provide a way of escape from enemies in times of danger.

This section of a new beaver canal was dug in one night. When a pond is occupied for a number of years the canals will be widened and deepened. Notice the neat manner in which the mud is piled on the bank.

129

A small, active beaver pond in Yellowstone National Park with a special feature, a beaver canal that is as straight as if a surveyor had laid out the route with a transit. Lodgepole Pines seem to be the only source of bark here.

This beaver canal is several feet wide, cuts through an area of quaking bog, connects two small lakes in the Massaweepie Boy Scout Camp at Gale, New York and is large enough to permit travel by canoe from one lake to the other.

These trails and roadways, after periods of heavy use, are most impressive, however, especially in places where they cross land that is low and wet. They often evolve into some of the most spectacular examples of beaver engineering achievements.

Canals

The canals that beavers dig are often far more impressive than the dams they build. Each canal has a simple beginning. During the course of a night, several yards of ditch may be dug inland from the edge of the pond, usually in an absolutely straight line, eighteen to twenty-four inches in width and approximately eighteen inches in depth, with the mud piled neatly along the sides. From that beginning, work continues on the canals as long as a pond is occupied. When a pond has been abandoned and later reoccupied, the old canals will be cleaned out, widened, and dug deeper. This work can go on for many years or even centuries in areas where beavers have been left undisturbed by man. Some of these old canals may be four or five feet wide, from three to four feet deep and several hundred feet in length. Some are wide enough, deep enough, and long enough to permit passage by canoe for considerable distance. These canals usually follow heavily used land routes, but they may also follow trickles and small streams of water to their sources.

A ditch dug by beavers to divert water into a pond which will be gradually deepened and widened until it becomes a full-sized canal.

131

The canals serve beavers well in a multitude of ways. They make it easier and safer to travel considerable distances inland and facilitate the transportation of materials too heavy to drag long distances over land. Many of these canals have dens dug into their banks where beavers can seek safety. Beaver canals are also used by many other forms of living things, including fish, amphibians, turtles, waterfowl, and muskrats.

Beaver Works in North American National Parks

Some of the best examples of the beaver's ability to alter conditions to suit his special needs may be found in some of the wide valleys that were once gouged out by glaciers with streams too swift to dam. In such locations beavers may dig channels that divert water from the main stream to fill a series of bypass ponds that terrace the valley for miles. One excellent example is in Rocky Mountain National Park, Estes Park, Colorado, at the headwaters of the Colorado River. Another

This is a series of bypass ponds on the west side of the Continental Divide near Silverton, Colorado where rapidly melting snow in the high country creates streams too swift for beavers to dam. Instead the beavers dig ditches to feed these bypass ponds. The ponds have been stocked with Eastern Brook Trout and provide excellent fishing.

132

An unusual beaver pond which is filled by water being pumped out of a silver mine near Silverton, Colorado.

is along a stream known as Mineral Creek between Ourey and Silverton, Colorado. In both places, the ponds have been stocked with Eastern Brook Trout and provide excellent fishing.

At the outskirts of Silverton, beavers built a long dam along the base of the mountain. The water that filled this one came from the shaft of a silver mine that was being pumped out.

On the other side of the mountain, a small watercourse ran down from the summit toward Ouray. Along this stream beavers built a series of small dams up the side of the mountain into the alpine meadow at the summit. These dams created a series of small water impoundments, many of them far above timber line. Examples of beaver works of this type are common in the mountains of the west. In every instance the works store water, retard erosion, and during brief summers, make it possible for beavers to graze on mountainsides and in lush alpine meadows. Near Cripple Creek, Colorado, a series of works of this type had willows growing out of the tops of the dams. In building them, the beavers had dragged brush upstream and used it in building the dams. In so doing, they established growths of trees on the side of the mountain above normal timberline.

133

The remnants of the two large dams in the foreground make excellent places for ducks, geese, and Trumpeter Swans to build their nests and incubate their eggs.

In Yellowstone National Park, beavers have been unmolested by man for well over a century; moreover, man removed cougars and wolves, the beaver's two chief predators. As a result, the beaver population rapidly increased to the carrying capacity of the range, but because of competition from the elk, the beaver population has been sharply reduced. Nevertheless, the extent of beaver works within the park is amazing. There are still many active ponds within the boundaries of the park, some of them very large, and the number of remnants of old dams in them attest to the former numbers and the extent of the works done by the beavers that once lived there. In addition to the active ponds, there are many large beaver meadows with dense growths of moose willows.

The name "moose willow" is most appropriate. These small trees get their name because they are heavily used by moose at every season of the year, but especially in winter when these thickets provide places for them to yard up and await the arrival of spring. These thickets provide not only food to sustain them but also provide protection from winter storms in an area where temperatures frequently drop well below −50° Fahrenheit. These old beaver meadows often offer an additional advantage. Because they are in a thermal area, the ground under them often remains warm. Yet another advantage is the absence of competition from elk during the winter. A large part of the summer herd migrates out of the park in the fall and spends the winter in the

Adult moose feeding on water lily sprouts in the bottom of the ponds in early spring.

National Elk Refuge in Jackson Hole, Wyoming. Elk offer little competition for the moose at any season of the year because they cannot digest and use willow as efficiently as moose. Moose can chew and digest willow twigs the size of a person's thumb, and for this reason the Algonquin Indians named him "the one who eats wood."

The first fresh food that the moose will find in the early spring will be sprouts of yellow pond lilies growing up from roots in the bottoms of beaver ponds with water that comes from hot springs. These ponds never freeze over, and lilies begin to sprout when the weather is still very cold. Sometimes moose will submerge themselves to get them. Water lilies constitute an important part of the diet of the moose as long as they are available.

Today, there are few new beaver ponds within the boundaries of Yellowstone National Park because elk browse on new sprouts as fast as they appear and make it most difficult for new growth to restore the stands of cottonwoods that were cut back in the days when beavers were plentiful and the elk few in number. There are, however, still a number of large ponds that are maintained, and these are used, not only by moose but by every species of waterfowl that breeds or winters in this area. Because of hot springs, some of them never freeze over, and on the coldest day of winter, flocks of Trumpeter Swans and Bufflehead Ducks swimming on the open water of a beaver pond are a common sight.

135

These Blacktail Beaver ponds are located in the Snake River Valley and are partially fed by hot springs so they never freeze over. Trumpeter Swans and Bufflehead Ducks use them in the winter because of the open water. The rest of the year ducks and moose come here to feed on water lilies. They also contain a large population of Cutthroat Trout.

THE BLACKTAIL PONDS

ONE ANIMAL SPECIES, BY ITS WAY OF LIFE, MAY CREATE HOMESITES FOR MANY OTHERS. HERE BEAVER HAVE DAMMED SPRING FED STREAMS FLOWING FROM THE BASE OF THE BLUFF. IN THE MARSH THUS FORMED, WILLOWS AND OTHER WETLAND PLANTS FLOURISH, PROVIDING FOOD AND SHELTER FOR MOOSE, MUSKRATS, MANY KINDS OF NESTING WATERFOWL AND A VARIETY OF SMALLER BIRDS. AN IDEAL WILDLIFE HABITAT HAS BEEN SO ESTABLISHED, ONE OF MANY SIMILAR AREAS ALONG THE SNAKE RIVER BOTTOMLANDS.

When Grand Teton National Park was created in 1929, the wildlife sanctuary area of Yellowstone National Park was enlarged by 310,576 acres, bringing the total area within the combined boundaries of the two parks to approximately 3954 square miles. This addition proved to be a boon to the beaver, for unlike Yellowstone where Lodgepole Pines predominate, Grand Teton National Park provides ideal conditions for the growth of aspens and cottonwoods. Beavers living here have another advantage over their Yellowstone counterparts in that they do not experience the degree of competition from elk.

The extent of the beaver work in Grand Teton National Park is impressive. Some of the ponds are extensive, and all are very interesting at any season of the year, but are especially so in spring. At that time, like those of Yellowstone, they provide prime nesting areas and places to raise young for large numbers and a wide variety of waterfowl. The evidence is in the numbers of mother ducks followed by flotillas of young that may be seen crossing and recrossing the surfaces of the ponds. These may include Barrow's Goldeneye, which nests in hollow trees. Any form of waterfowl whose breeding range extends over the area will be well represented in the parks. Trumpeter Swans and Canada Geese often take advantage of the works of the beavers by building nests on the tops of their houses. One stand of cottonwoods in the vicinity of the Snake River provides a nesting place for a number of Great Blue Herons that make regular trips to and from the beaver ponds.

A pair of Trumpeter Swans with the nest they built on the top of a muskrat house in a beaver pond.

One of several unusually large cottonwood trees cut down by beavers along the Snake River in Grand Teton National Park, Moose, Wyoming. All the trees were at least three feet in diameter, this one measured approximately 44 inches at the stump, shown contrasting with the hat which is 14½ inches in diameter.

In another locality near the river, beavers cut down a row of large poplars. The smallest had a trunk diameter of over twenty-four inches, and the stump of the largest was estimated to be forty-four inches across. In the vicinity of the logs of the large trees, another large one, dead but still standing, was in the middle of a small abandoned beaver pond. Bald Eagles chose the top of this tree as a place to build their nest and returned to it to rear their young year after year.

From Colorado north to the Canadian National Parks of Banff, Jasper, and beyond, there are many very interesting and unusual works of beavers. Beavers use the world-famous lakes of the Canadian National Parks freely, building ponds around them. Many of the lakes, like those of Yellowstone and the Tetons, are fed by hot springs, are never completely frozen over, and provide winter havens for Trumpeter Swans and wintering ducks.

In summer these ponds provide places for Trumpeter Swans, Canada Geese, ducks, and other forms of waterfowl to raise their young. They also provide lush growths of yellow water lilies that are a favorite food of the moose, and when a pond is recently drained, animals, including bands of ewes and lambs of Bighorn Sheep, come there to get minerals.

On the eastern slopes of the Rockies there are many areas that have been designated as National Forests, when in fact they support

The only twin beaver houses ever seen by the author were these in a pond on the Pennsylvania side of the Delaware River near Callicoon, New York. Apparently a pair of beaver each built their own house and spent the winter in it.

very few or no trees. It is in these areas that ranchers are permitted to graze their cattle and sheep, and here beavers have also become established. The ponds that they build are as heavily used by waterfowl as the prairie potholes are further east.

The large quantities of sticks, poles, and small logs that may be seen on the downstream side of a large beaver dam attest to the fact that over a period of years a family of beavers cuts down a large number of trees and saplings. The number of poles and small logs with bark still on them that can be seen in this type of dam is also strong evidence that a large amount of material is not cut to furnish food. The most intensive cutting is done during the early stages of dam building and house construction.

Where available, alders are the most frequently used building materials, and an alder thicket furnishes a convenient and abundant supply. They grow in thick clumps in wet areas, and each trunk is approximately two inches or less in diameter at the base. These are cut, the leaves and small twigs are eaten, and the unpeeled poles are either added to the downstream side of the dam or dragged up on the side of the house. When a new pond is being established, cutting is begun in the spring and continues all summer. Once a family has become established, it is peeled sticks that most frequently appear on the downstream side of the dam. When seeking to locate live beaver ponds

139

from the air, investigators look for the presence of "white wood" on the dam or house.

In a well-established location, little cutting is done during the spring and summer, for that is the time when a varied and abundant food supply is available. Cutting for the storing of food usually begins at about the time the leaves begin to turn color, and it continues at an accelerated pace until ice locks in the pond.

Studies conducted with captive beavers in Michigan conclude that one acre of small poplar saplings will support a single beaver for seven years or seven beavers for one year (6). Actually, under natural conditions considerably larger amounts of material are cut. Where beavers have been living in a place for a number of years, the members in a family may average from six to ten and possibly more. On the basis of seven beavers in a family and one acre of land cleared in a year, we get a rough idea of the extent of a cleared area over a period of time.

Beavers do not do clear cutting. They tend to distribute their activities to the most convenient locations. However, when they cut a tree or sapling, an area is cleared around it. To the average person, one acre of land is a vague unit of measurement. To learn that an acre is 4840 square yards may be of little help. However, the playing area of a football field is 100 yards long and 50 yards wide, for a total area of 5000 square yards, or slightly more than an acre.

The rate of new tree growth cannot begin to keep pace with the rate of cutting. Every year, members of the family must travel farther inland to find suitable stands of trees. Small-diameter sticks and poles of any species may be stripped completely of their bark, but a larger proportion of smooth-bark trees such as aspens, poplars, beech, birches, and Blue Beech are utilized. It is not unusual to see six-inch diameter lengths of logs of these species of trees with the bark completely peeled from them.

As long as a pond is occupied, members of the beaver family must travel inland to do their cutting, and when stands of timber within convenient distances from the pond are used up, it requires longer travel over land, it is more difficult to transport material back to the pond, and there is a greatly increased risk of attacks by enemies that may get between them and the safety of the water. When it becomes necessary to travel too great a distance from the ponds to do their cutting, entire families usually move out to seek more favorable places to live.

5

The Life Cycle of a Beaver Pond

When a pair of beavers moves in and occupies a territory, the effects upon the environment are far reaching. The lands east of the Mississippi were once prime beaver country, and there we may find a typical situation where a pair of pioneering beavers might choose to live. As long as they live there, they make many changes in their environment, and their works affect the lives of many other creatures, but after they leave, nature moves in to reclaim it.

In that type of environment there are typically valleys where small streams flow through thickets of alders. In places where banks are higher, there may be an occasional Red Maple, willow, or sycamore. Flanking these alder thickets may be stands of Quaking Aspens. This is also a situation favorable for the growth of Eastern Cottonwoods and Bigtooth Aspens. Higher up on the hillsides there may be volunteer growths of ash, hard maple, and Yellow Birch from seeds that were dispersed by the wind, and oaks, hickories, Butternut, and Black Walnut planted by Gray Squirrels. In old woodlots, around former home sites, and along abandoned roads there may be a number of old trees that are partly hollow and thus well suited to serve as nesting places and den trees. There may also be blocks of pines, spruces, and larches that were planted by members of the Civilian Conservation Corps during the years of the Depression. This type of situation invites the return of the beaver.

A beaver pond goes through a series of stages, each reflecting the changes brought about by the beaver's manipulation of his environment. These stages may be likened to those of life, for indeed, the beaver pond can be viewed as a living, changing, and growing thing. It progress from birth through infancy, adolescence, maturity, old age, and eventually death, or abandonment. We may use this framework here for considering the life cycle of a beaver pond in the river valley just described.

141

Birth

The first beaver to move into this type of situation might well be a young adult that has been driven from the family group after its second winter, the time of its expulsion probably early March. He may have wandered many miles before he found a suitable location that was not occupied.

The young outcast that moves into the valley may possibly be the first of his kind to be found there for over two centuries. When he arrives, he finds an ample supply of water, an abundance and wide variety of good things to eat, and a source of building materials that will last for many years. Best of all, he occupies territory that is unclaimed and unused by other families of beavers. The former outcast becomes a true beaver pioneer. He finds a favorite resting place a short distance upstream from an alder thicket where the current has undercut the bank beneath the roots of a medium-size Red Maple. There he finds shade, shelter, and concealment, but he may not be content with conditions as he finds them so he digs out a den that becomes his chief living quarters during the summer. For the most part he lives the carefree life of a bachelor beaver and spends his time, eating, sleeping, and exploring.

In his travels, from time to time, he stops to build up piles of mud. On these mud pies he places his signature in the form of a few drops

A fresh sign heap made by beavers to mark the boundaries of their territory. They are usually made of mud but sphagnum moss or other materials may be used as appears to have been the case here. When completed, the beaver stakes his claim with a few drops of castoreum from the musk glands placed on the heap.

from his castor glands, and by so doing he marks out the boundaries of his territory and proclaims the fact that he is prepared to defend it. He does one thing more. In a location downstream from the alder thicket he finds a place where the banks were narrow. To this spot he drags alder brush, weights it down with stones, plasters the upstream side with mud, and builds a small dam which backs up water to the tops of the banks. When this is done, it is possible to do some traveling by water, and it also provides a measure of safety.

There comes a day when a second young adult beaver that has wandered many miles in search of a place to live arrives in the valley, this one a female, and for the resident, his bachelor days are at an end. He has found a mate, and with a pair present, there will be many changes in the valley for years to come.

Even after the arrival of the second beaver, changes come very slowly during the first summer. Except for an occasional stump to mark the spot where a piece of brush has been cut or the sight of freshly peeled sticks that appear in the small dam, or when the stream runs muddy when it should be clear, there is little evidence to confirm the presence of a pair of beavers.

Back in the middle of the alder thicket, however, on a spot of slightly higher ground, there is a favorite eating spot. Around it there accumulates a number of peeled sticks. By mid-September, when days

A night picture of a beaver working on its dam at France Brook, Allegany State Park, Red House, New York.

143

A completed beaver house large enough in which to spend the winter. Notice the number of sticks on top of the house used in the construction and a good number of sticks protruding from the water near the house, indicating a stocked food pile ready for winter.

began to grow shorter, these sticks are stacked in a pile with the center hollowed out. On top of it are piled poles of alder, and work on the house begins in earnest. The long poles give it the general shape of a broad-based teepee. In the meantime, the living quarters inside are enlarged by cutting away the ceiling. When the room is large enough, the outside of the house is plastered with layer upon layer of mud, and the house has well-constructed tunnels as places of entrance and exit. However, when the leaves are still on the alders, the house is well concealed within the thicket.

When the leaves begin to turn color, there is a sharp increase in the pace of activity. Work begins in the later afternoon and continues during the night until well after daybreak. The house is enlarged somewhat, but most of the work is concentrated on the dam. The height is raised approximately a foot, and the length extends to over fifty feet. The alder thicket provides an abundant and convenient source of building material in the form of poles with butt diameters of from two to three inches. While this is going on, a muskrat that was flooded out of the hole in the bank where it has been living digs a snug den into the side of the beaver house and moves in. Work continues at

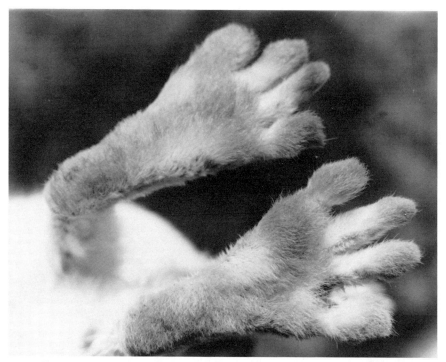

Closeup view of the bottoms of the feet of a Snowshoe Hare showing the stiff, white hairs beginning to grow between the toes of the hugh hind feet with the approach of cold weather, creating a highly efficient pair of snowshoes.

a rapid pace until cold weather moves in and the pond freezes over. Then all work stops abruptly. A most unusual feature of this new pond is the absence of the usual food pile that beavers store up for the winter.

The first winter is unusually severe. A thick layer of ice covers the new pond, and on it lies a deep blanket of snow. The only outward sign of life below is the whisp of steam that sometimes rises from the "chimney" of the house on a cold clear day.

Other forms of wildlife that have long been absent begin to return to the valley. Of special interest one of these makes frequent nightly visits to the vicinity of the new beaver pond, and wherever he goes, he leaves behind a complete record of his travels in the form of distinct sets of footprints in the snow. This one might well be called, "the rabbit that runs on snowshoes," a name which fits him exceptionally well. When the snows lie deep in the woods, he goes bounding over the tops of the snow banks while heavier bodied enemies sink in and fall behind. He is generally known as the Varying Hare or Snowshoe Hare and is sometimes referred to as the white rabbit.

145

Snowshoe Hare in an early snowfall with its coat beginning to turn to white for winter. The beaver survives by changing its surroundings to suit its needs and the hare succeeds in surviving by going to extremes to adapt itself to changing conditions. In addition to the color change with the seasons and the snowshoes, it has a digestive system that any goat would envy, and thrives on low-grade foods like spruce, where a deer would starve.

Both the hare and the beaver thrive in wilderness conditions that are sometimes exceedingly harsh, but for opposite reasons: the beaver, because of his ability to change his environment to suit his special needs, and the hare because of his unique ability to adapt himself to the changing conditions of his environment. Nature gives him two coats a year, a summer coat of brownish gray and a warm winter overcoat of white that matches the landscape of the winter's snow.

The Snowshoe Hare is larger than the Eastern or New England Cottontail Rabbit, and his summer coat is somewhat darker in color, but he can easily be told from the cottontail at any season of the year by the size of the heavily muscled hind legs and especially by the huge hind feet. Unlike baby cottontails that are born blind and helpless, baby Snowshoe Hares are born fully furred and can walk the day they are born. By the time they are ten days old, they are half grown and at thirty days, fully grown.

By the time leaves begin to turn color in the fall, changes also begin to take place with the varying hare. Stiff white hairs begin to grow between his toes and on the bottoms of his feet. Then his feet turn white, and rings of white appear around his eyes. By the time the first snow falls, he is no longer brown but spotted brown on his back and white around his underparts. By the time the ground is covered with a

146

Upper right: Adult Snowshoe Hare with a full coat of white winter fur. The Snowshoe Hare shares a large part of its northern range, where the winters are long and hard, with the beaver. Above: A Snowshoe Hare in March with its fur coat rapidly changing to brown for summer which makes good cover in the shadows. Right: A Snowshoe Hare in April with the fur completely changed to its summer coat of brown.

blanket of snow, the hare has completely put on his winter overcoat of white. He shares with the beaver the ability to thrive on a great variety of low-grade foods and grow fat in a spruce thicket where a deer would starve.

Another creature that is returning to abandoned farm country is the Ruffed Grouse. This bird is also especially adapted to survive under harsh winter conditions. It feeds chiefly on the buds of trees, and it also grows "snowshoes" on its feet, for as the days grow shorter in the fall, feathers grow out between the toes. The grouse takes refuge from the cold and confuses predators by diving into a snowbank during a storm and letting the wind blow over its back and cover it up. Outside blizzards may rage, fierce winds may howl, and temperatures may drop to −40° and below, yet the bird insulated by a coat of feathers remains warm and snug in its "form" in the snow.

147

Infancy

For many weeks a heavy blanket of snow covers the hills and the floor of the valley, but an early return of spring brings a combination of unseasonably warm weather combined with unusually heavy rains. The heavy blanket of snow is thus turned into a torrent of water which rushes down the valley and flows over the top of the dam. The dam sustains damage, but on the whole it withstands the onslaught extremely well. It also spreads out the flood waters, slows them down, and reduces their power to do damage farther downstream. When the flood subsides, the beavers soon repair the breaks in the dam.

The flood does little damage to the dam, but it results in sudden and drastic changes in the appearance of the pond. The beavers have freely cut and used the alders in the building of the house and the construction of the dam, but there are many clumps that remain standing, apparently undisturbed during the winter. The flood waters topple these over and sweep some of them over the dam and out of the pond. Others are lodged along the top of the dam.

Alders normally withstand flash floods exceptionally well. The reason for this aberration is evident as soon as the high waters recede. During the winter the beavers cut off, dug up, and ate the roots and in the process completely dug up the pond bottom.

The first warm, rainy night of early April brings hundreds of Spotted and Jefferson Salamanders up from the places underground where they spent the winter. They slither down the hillsides into the quiet backwaters of the beaver pond, and there they find expanded and ideal conditions for attaching their gelatin-encased egg masses to submerged twigs. These eggs later hatch into fishlike tadpoles with external gills. When these are replaced by lungs a few weeks later, the young salamanders return to land. Thereafter they live out their lives on land except during the few days each spring when they return to water to lay their eggs.

Salamanders are not the only creatures to seek out the quiet backwaters of the pond. The first arrivals to proclaim their presence are the tiny Swamp Cricket Frogs. A few tentative voices at first, then more and more tiny songsters added their elfin voices to swell the chorus until it can be heard for a half mile on a warm spring evening. Soon, other voices join the chorus with single piercing, high-pitched notes that lack the trill of those of the Cricket Frogs. These are the first voices of the Spring Peepers. Both the Cricket Frogs and the Spring Peepers are tiny creatures with body lengths seldom exceeding an inch and a quarter, yet the sounds they make can be heard for long distances. Their markings are quite different. The Cricket Frog has three irregular stripes down its back, while the back of the Spring Peeper is distinctly marked with an X-shaped cross.

Baby Snowshoe Hare, five days old.

Swamp Cricket Frog, *Pseudacris tricereata*. The first voice of spring, even earlier than the spring peeper, *Hyla crucifer*, belongs to the Swamp Cricket Frog. The flooded backwater of a new beaver pond will be filled with these tiny songsters, which measure only a little over an inch in body length.

Wood Frog, *Rana sylvatica*. As the name implies, the Wood Frog is a creature of wooded areas. It lays eggs in temporary pools in early spring and is quick to find and use the flooded backwaters provided by beavers, especially in heavily wooded areas. The eggs hatch quickly, and the tadpoles develop rapidly. Wood Frogs are usually fawn colored and have a black line across the eyes. They feed chiefly on insects they find on the forest floor.

149

Leopard Frog, *Rana pipiens*. Beaver ponds, especially new ones, make ideal places for Leopard Frogs to lay their eggs and the tadpoles to develop. The deep green coat with the roundish spots are distinctive makings. However, this frog has the ability to change its color and during the egg-laying season the background may be greenish brown.

As water temperatures rise, the choruses of Cricket Frogs and Spring Peepers are replaced by the strident cackling of Wood Frogs that congregate in the shallows to lay their eggs. These in turn are replaced by the guttural sounds of Leopard Frogs.

Even before the last of the Leopard Frogs have laid their eggs, a common sound of the night, especially on a warm, rainy one, is the loud trill of the Tree Toad. Unlike the other toads and frogs that spend most of their time on the land, this one, as its name implies, is adapted to life in the trees. It is equipped with vacuum cups on the tips of its toes which give it a firm grip when climbing and the remarkable ability to change its color from gray to various shades of green and back in a very short time, to match the colors of its surroundings.

By the time that buds begin to burst on the trees and blades of grass start to rise, the choruses of these tiny songsters of the early spring are replaced by the rich, full alto sounds of the Common Toads that assemble there to find mates and lay strings of eggs on the bottom of the pond before they return to land.

While the toads are laying their eggs, a turtle might sometimes be seen basking in the sunlight on a moss-covered bank. This one has an upper shell that is covered with bright yellow spots. The Spotted Turtle was once a common creature of the swampy woods, but it is becoming increasingly rare and is now seldom seen. When seen resting on the

150

Male Wood Duck in breeding plumage. The make Wood Duck is often referred to as the peacock of all waterfowl. There is a most interesting association between the beaver, the Pileated Woodpecker and the Wood Duck. The beaver backs up water that kills trees and the Pileated Woodpecker chisels out nesting holes in the trees. When they are abandoned by the woodpeckers, they are ideal places for Wood Ducks to build their nests and lay their eggs.

bank, the reason for the spots is not apparent, but in a woodland pool covered with duckweed, they provide perfect camouflage.

In the meantime myriads of tiny black tadpoles emerge from egg masses, spread out, and find abundant sources of food amid decaying vegetation on the bottom of the pond. With the abundance of food available, they grow and mature rapidly. The beavers build the dam and make a pond, but in so doing, they create a food pyramid with a very broad base.

A pair of Wood Ducks flies into the valley early in the spring, finds the pond, and remain in the area. The male Wood Duck is often called "the peacock of all waterfowl," for when in full breeding plumage, he is a creature of rare beauty. His more somber-colored mate blends perfectly with the background of a wooded area whether in the trees or on the ground. Wood Ducks are as much at home in the woodlands as the Ruffed Grouse. They feed on a great variety of fruits and berries, and when there is a crop of beechnuts, they feast on them. They climb

151

among the branches of white oak trees and gather acorns, and they can even swallow and grind up hickory nuts in their gizzards.

The female Wood Duck nests in hollows in trees, and she can squeeze her body through a small opening. A favorite nesting place is the abandoned nest of a Pileated Woodpecker. The pair diligently searches the area in the vicinity of the pond but finds no suitable nesting tree. About half a mile distant in a former farm woodlot is a stand of large beech trees in some of which high branches have broken off, and hollows have formed behind them.

After exploring a number of these, the Wood Ducks select one that seems to have an opening and cavity of proper dimensions. For a number of days thereafter, the female makes repeated trips to this site. She pulls feathers from her breast to line the nest and then lays twelve cream-colored eggs. In her trips to and from the nesting tree she never follows a direct route, and when she approaches the nesting tree, she sets her wings and dives directly into the hole. Incubation is done by the female, and it may last from twenty-eight to thirty-four days.

When the young are fully developed, they make use of a special tool that nature has provided: the egg tooth at the tip of the bill whose sole purpose is to enable the duckling to cut through the egg shell. Once that is done, they push the shells aside and kick themselves free. At first they are weak, wet, and wobbly, but they rapidly dry out and gain strength. When all are hatched and ready to travel, their mother begins to call and coax them out from the nesting cavity. One by one, they climb out of the cavity and stand on the edge of the hole until each summons the courage to jump. When they do, they land right as corks, uninjured by a twenty-foot drop. When the last downy duckling has jumped, they line up behind their mother at evenly spaced intervals and follow her down to the pond. It is small at first, but as the ducklings increase in size, so does the pond. By their works, the beavers have created ideal conditions for the Wood Ducks to return to the valley for the first time in many years.

During the winter the beavers mated, and approximately one hundred days later two young are born early in May. The number in a litter usually varies from two to four, sometimes more, but two is normal for the first litter. The kits are born fully furred, their eyes are open, and the teeth are well developed. They also have the distinctive paddle-like tails. At birth they weigh approximately one pound each. At about the same time four baby muskrats are born inside the den that had been dug into the side of the beaver house. In contrast with the beaver kits, these are born blind and helpless, and it is several days before their eyes are open.

The house that sheltered the pair during the winter rapidly becomes too small for the growing family. The male moves out when

Beaver house in late summer when the water is low, note the top of the entrance tunnel just left of center.

the kits are small and goes back to live in the bank burrow under the roots of the Red Maple, but he returns to the pond every afternoon. There is much work to be done. The growing family needs a larger pond and a house with more room inside. Despite the demands on the female for taking care of her young, both adults work long hours. Work usually starts in the late afternoon and continues through the night until sunup. More sticks and more poles are piled on the outside of the lodge, and the inside chamber is enlarged by cutting away material from the ceiling to make it higher and from the sides to make it wider. This material is tramped under foot and raises the floor above the rising water level of the pond. When completed, the floor is carpeted with finely shredded wood.

Work on the dam goes on continuously. It is made higher, longer, and stronger by the sticks and poles laid on the downstream side and the mud dredged up from the bottom and plastered against the upstream side.

As soon as work is well started on the main dam, form one to several secondary dams may also be under construction. These relieve the pressure on the main dam and also increase the distance that the beavers can travel up- and downstream by water.

Whitetail Deer disappeared from the area early in the nineteenth century and did not begin to return until the first quarter of the twentieth. At about the time that the baby beavers are born, proof

153

of the presence of deer appears in the form of a doe that has come out of the woods and given birth to twin fawns. She places them in separate locations a considerable distance apart. Each lies motionless and almost invisible because its spotted coat blends so perfectly with its surroundings. In the early days of its life the fawn has additional protection. It has no body odor whereby a predator might detect its presence. When they are rested and have enough strength to travel, the doe returns, and they follow her back into the woods on rubbery little legs. This is the first trip of the doe to the vicinity of the pond, but it will not be the last. She and her fawns will be regular visitors.

As the beavers increase the area of the pond, they broaden the base of the food pyramid within it. Bacteria rapidly break down dead vegetation, and they, in turn, are eaten by protozoa, which are then food for a host of other creatures. The bottom and edges of the pond support a teeming mass of life: cyclops, daphnia, or water fleas, and shrimp-like *Gammarus*. Mosquitoes find the pond and lay their eggs which rapidly develop into mosquito wigglers. These are avidly consumed by the baby Wood Ducks. Tadpoles of Cricket Frogs, Spring Peepers, Wood Frogs, Tree Toads, and Common Toads absorb their tails, grow legs, develop lungs and come out on the land where they

Tree Toad, *Hyla versicolor*, or "Sticky Toes." The Tree Toad is an early user of new beaver ponds, and loud choruses of these interesting creatures can be heard around such places on warm spring nights. They have vacuum cups on their toes, and they can climb up smooth surfaces, even panes of glass.

154

A night picture of a beaver swimming across the pond towing brush to stock the food pile.

feed upon the swarms of mosquitoes and other tiny insects that have developed in the pond.

Tree Swallows skim across the surface of the water in a quest for emerging hatches of insects. Dragonflies and Damsel Flies are attracted to the pond for the abundance of flying insects and for a place to lay their eggs.

Brook Trout managed to survive in the creek, but they were few in number and small in size. Many generations had lived out their lives and managed to reproduce without getting to be over five inches in length. Suddenly in the pond they have all the food that they can eat in the form of aquatic insects, Caddice Worms, *Gammarus*, (freshwater shrimp), and fat tadpoles. Runted trout grow hog fat, doubling and redoubling their weights. Tiny sticklebacks gorge themselves on mosquito wigglers as do schools of small minnows.

Beaver kits are weaned at approximately six weeks, but they begin to take solid food much earlier. The female makes trip after trip from the house and returns with freshly cut twigs and grasses. In spite of the repeated trips she makes, the little ones are always hungry, and they are most vociferous and insistent in their demands for food. Their strident voices can be heard at a considerable distance from the house.

A beaver kit swimming.

When they are weaned, they weigh approximately four pounds each, or four times their birth weight.

Baby beavers can swim at an early age, but unfortunately they float like corks, cannot dive, and are easy prey for a large owl or hawk. There are times when the price of survival may be the ability to dive fast and deep combined with the ability to stay under water until the danger has passed. When the female brings the kits out, at first they do not venture far from the safety of the house, but each day they go farther. In the meantime, the male joins the family group.

At about the time the kits made regular excursions out of the house, there is a mass exodus from the pond in the form of thousands upon thousands of little Leopard Frogs that have transformed from tadpoles. Some are still in the stump-tail stage when they leave the water. They immediately begin to feed upon the swarms of insects that have spent their larval stages in the water and are beginning to hatch.

There are other changes in the pond. The male Wood Duck that so proudly displayed his gorgeous breeding colors in the early spring is in eclipse plumage, furtive and flightless. When he molted, he lost his flight feathers and took time to grow in new ones. In appearance he

156

now resembles the female. She too is flightless, but she escorts her flotilla of rapidly growing ducklings on a constant search of good things to eat.

One reason for the rapid growth of the ducklings is the abundance of a tiny floating green plant, appropriately known as duckweed. It reproduces rapidly until it completely covers a pond. The plant is approximately one-fifth of an inch in diameter, has roots, and despite its very small size, it is a flowering plant. Waterfowl consume it avidly, and the spatulate bills of ducks are admirably adapted for scooping it up. Beavers and muskrats also consume it in large quantities. As the animals float along the surface, they push it into their mouths with their front feet.

For the beaver family, late spring and early summer are a time of leisurely living. Work on the dam and the house never stops, but it does proceed at a slower pace. They are surrounded by an abundance of good things to eat, and it is seldom necessary to venture far from the

A night picture of a beaver at the edge of a pond.

pond to find them. In addition to the duckweed there are grasses, fruits, and mushrooms. Little cutting is done except when it is necessary to chew on something hard to keep their incisor teeth worn down and sharpened. Their chief activity is eating, and as a result they grow rapidly at summer's end. The adults approach weights of fifty pounds each, and the kits, about fifteen pounds each.

The Wood Duck ducklings not only increase rapidly in size, but like the adults they are growing in their feathers and are beginning to make short flights.

As the season advances, activities in and around the pond increase. The dam is made higher, tighter, and stronger. The height is raised about a foot, and it doubles in length. The house that was once concealed in an alder thicket now stands alone in the pond, and every day the layers of mud are plastered on the outside until it resembles a Navajo hogan.

A newly enlarged beaver house, plastered and readied for winter, looking a lot like a Navajo hogan.

Night picture of a beaver swimming with a chunk of a small tree trunk for the food pile, or perhaps for some repairs on the dam.

Brook Trout require an area where clean well-oxygenated water flows over a gravel bottom as a place to spawn. Wherever water is backed up behind the beaver dams, these spawning conditions do not exist, but these places do supply an abundance of things to eat that never existed there before. When it is spawning time for the Brook Trout, they take on their gorgeous breeding colors and travel upstream until they find a suitable place to spawn, and they then return to the pond where food is plentiful.

In the space of a few months, many changes have taken place. The house has more than doubled in size. The pond is larger, the dam longer, and the family has doubled in numbers with a corresponding increase in the family's food requirements. As a result, work on the food pile starts early. Materials to add to it are abundant and close at hand. The pond is partially surrounded by Quaking Aspens that are easily cut and lean naturally toward the pond, and most fall into the water where they are cut up and towed away. In some instances the trunks of small diameter are cut into evenly spaced lengths that are either added to the food pile or thrown out over the dam. Work never stops until the pond is locked in by ice.

While these preparations are in progress, the doe and her twin fawns make regular visits to the pond. All are in full winter coats, and the fawns are nearly as large as their mother. The deer family

159

Beaver house and pond in winter with snow drifted deep on the ground.

frequently takes advantage of the beavers' work by eating the buds from the aspen that the beavers have cut down before they have an opportunity to trim and drag the limbs away.

As days became colder, the Wood Ducks became increasingly restless, and one day they take off from the pond, headed south. The first ice begins to form late in November, and the heavy snow arrives in the form of several storms in late December. The beaver family is well prepared to spend the winter.

In building the food pile they have amassed so much material that a considerable amount is above the level of the ice and snow. This is discovered by the keen nose of a Snowshoe Hare in full winter coat with fully developed snowshoes on his feet. He makes regular trips to the pile to dine upon buds and bark. His presence does not go unnoticed, however. One night a bobcat begins to stalk him from the opposite side of the beaver house. At a critical instant, the hare stands up, sniffs the air, and takes off in full flight with the bobcat in close pursuit. In deep snow, the bobcat rapidly falls behind. Nature did not provide him with snowshoes as she did his cousin, the lynx.

Adolescence

After spring breakup time, salamanders, Cricket Frogs, Spring Peepers, Wood Frogs, Leopard Frogs, Tree Toads, and Common Toads

160

concentrate in selected areas to lay their eggs as the water attains proper temperatures as they did the year before, but this year there is a difference. Several Wild Turkeys descend from the oak ridges and hillsides at the time that the Leopard Frogs are laying their eggs. They wade into the pond up to their bellies, snatch up, and swallow frogs as fast as they can catch them. When they leave, they are full fed for the first time in many weeks. Their raids decimate the concentration of Leopard Frogs, and there are fewer eggs left to hatch than the year before.

Wild Turkeys disappeared by 1830 and did not return until the middle of the next century. As with the White-tailed Deer and the Beaver, the Wild Turkey was brought back because of the enlightened self-interest of organized sportsmen.

Migrating American Woodcocks drop in and find the soft earth at the edge of the pond an ideal place to probe for earthworms. Some decide to stay, lay their eggs, and rear their young.

The Wild Turkey has made a strong comeback with the help of a successful trap-and-transfer program and the restoration of some forested areas. The clearings around beaver ponds make ideal locations for the poults to find high-grade protein in the form of grasshoppers and other insects, and in the early spring, adults will wade into shallow water to catch and eat frogs that have come to lay their eggs.

Young raccoon up a tree. The raccoon was once very rare animal but is now very common. It is completely omnivorous and in many instances a most serious predator. It destroys many nests of duck eggs as well as those of other birds and Snapping Turtles.

Blossoms of the aspens and poplars are a favorite early spring food of the Ruffed Grouse and as long as they are available, Ruffed Grouse congregate in the valley to feed on them. The Wood Ducks have managed to survive the perils of migration travel and the winter months. They arrive early, search out, find, and reoccupy the nesting hole that they successfully used the year before.

A flock of Black Ducks drops in. One pair finds the pond surrounded by woodlands an ideal location to rear a brood of young, and they set out in search of a suitable location to make a nest. A pair of northbound Hooded Mergansers passing high overhead looks down and discovers the pond, circles down, and lands. There they find that it supports a healthy population of fish. They decide to stay and set out in search of a tree with a nesting hole similar to the one used by the Wood Ducks. Fortunately, they find one without coming in conflict with the Wood Ducks.

Evidence of the rapid transition from terrestrial to aquatic forms of life appears in the form of midland painted turtles which climb onto logs to sun themselves. Of necessity, they have traveled considerable distances to find the pond.

One afternoon a Snapping Turtle crawls out of the pond, travels a short distance inland, digs a hole, lays a clutch of eggs, covers them, and returns to the water. That night a prowling raccoon comes that way, sniffs out their location, digs them up, and eats them. On land or

162

Dead tree showing an abandoned woodpecker hole which will in turn be used by Tree Swallows, Wood Ducks, Hooded Mergansers, Screech Owls or Kestrels.

in the trees, raccoons seek out duck nests and rob them. In the water, Snapping Turtles pull down swimming ducks, drown, and eat them. Raccoons and the Snapping Turtles are chief predators of ducks and other waterfowl, but in this instance, the raccoon has performed a service to waterfowl by reducing the potential population of another predator, the Snapping Turtle.

The water that backed up behind the dam flooded the land and killed the trees that were standing in the pond, and immediately the forces of decay began to attack them. Bacteria, fungi, and larvae of wood-boring insects begin to break them down and consume them. Woodpeckers chip and chisel away wood in search of grubs. In addition to serving as places to search for food, dead tree trunks make ideal places for woodpeckers to excavate nesting holes. The crow-sized Pileated Woodpecker which had long been rare in the valley becomes more common and chisels out the characteristic squarish nesting holes in trunks of large dead trees. As gravity and wind break off dead limbs, beavers drag them away to use on the house or in the dam.

The relationship between Beavers, Pileated Woodpeckers, and Wood Ducks has been a longstanding one. Beavers build dams that back up water and kill trees, and Pileated Woodpeckers chisel out nesting holes in them. When they are abandoned by the woodpeckers,

163

Beaver swimming close to the dam during the summer after a long period without rain. Notice the water level in the pond was at least two feet below the top of the dam pictured in the background.

they make ideal nesting holes for Wood Ducks. In the pond the nests are seldom disturbed by climbing predators, and when the ducklings hatch, they can drop down into the water without making a dangerous overland journey.

Other woodpeckers also take advantage of dead trees as places to chisel out nesting holes. The Yellow-shafted Flicker, the Red-bellied, Hairy, Downy, and Red-headed Woodpeckers, and Yellow-bellied Sapsuckers all raise their young in cavities they excavate in dead trees, and because of their smaller size they can use trees that are too small for the Pileated Woodpeckers.

Abandoned woodpecker holes are used by many other forms of birds and wildlife, and abandoned flicker holes are large enough to provide nesting cavities for Screech Owls, Saw-whet Owls, and kestrels. Abandoned nests of small woodpeckers provide ideal homes for Tree Swallows and Blue Birds. Abandoned woodpecker holes furnish homes for mice, chipmunks, and squirrels.

At about the middle of May, the beaver population doubles again. Four kits are born, and as he did the year before, the male moves out and lives apart until the kits are weaned. In less than three years the family has grown from the pioneering pair that moved into the valley to a family group consisting of a pair of adults, two subadults, and four rapidly growing kits.

164

A growing beaver family needs larger living quarters, and toward this end, sticks and poles are piled up on the outside while the ceiling and sides of the chamber are chiselled out on the inside. In addition to the need for larger living quarters, the family food requirements also sharply increase. The year before duckweed was a chief source of food. It was abundant, convenient, and nutritious. It lay in a mat that covered the surface of the pond, and it was only necessary for members of the beaver family to float around and stuff it into their mouths with their front feet. This year there are not only twice as many beavers to consume it but also more ducks and numerous families of muskrats. As a result duckweed is being consumed faster than it can reproduce itself. Consequently, the members of the beaver family do more feeding on the land than they did the year before. There they find an abundance of grasses and forbs growing near the water, and there are also shrubs and saplings close at hand.

The dam receives unusual attention, and work on it progresses without interruption from spring breakup time until ice covers the

Mature beaver pond in October after a very dry summer; except for the water in this pond, the creek was almost dry. The beavers have started to build up the food pile for winter, shown in the center of the photo.

Large house readied for winter with a large well stocked food pile to the right of the house, where the sticks can be seen poking out of the water.

pond. This year there are more workers making contributions, for in addition to the original pair, the subadults are beginning to learn "to work like beavers." The height of the dam is raised by another foot and made longer accordingly. This proves to be the maximum height of the dam and depth and size of the pond. In future years work on the dam will not stop as long as the pond is occupied. It will be built thicker and stronger but never higher. Before winter sets in, places that were dry land when the first beavers moved in are pond bottom covered with five to six feet of water.

Work on the house never stops during the summer. Sticks and poles are stacked on it until it becomes a huge dome-shaped wood pile twenty feet across at the base and over four feet above the surface of the water. By the time that the leaves begin to change color, layer upon layer of mud is plastered on it until all of the stick work is completely covered.

Work on the food pile begins early and proceeds at an increasingly rapid rate. It is practically the sole source of sustenance for eight beavers from mid-December until spring breakup time in March. When the pond was started, it stood in the middle of a wooded area. This year the beaver family has cut down over an acre of trees, mostly aspens and poplars with trunk diameters of from six to eight inches. As the trees are felled, branches are cut into convenient lengths, dragged into the pond, and added to the food pile. Tree trunks of moderate diameter that lay near the water are sometimes also used.

Cutting larger diameter trees is a wasteful operation. Beavers are able to utilize a rather small portion of the trees they fell. One result of the cutting is that the pond that was in the middle of a wooded area is now surrounded by a clearing.

A large Eastern Cottonwood Tree which has been attacked by beavers twice. The beavers partially cut it and quit. The tree started to heal itself and the fresh tooth marks on the new growth are evidence that beavers started to work on the tree again.

167

Green Frog, *Rana clamitans*. The Green Frog can be distinguished from the Bullfrog not only by its smaller size but also by the two distinctive wrinkles of skin down the sides of its back. This frog always lives close to the water and beaver ponds are ideal because it takes over a year for the tadpoles to develop into mature frogs.

During the third winter, there are times when members of the family go to the edge of the pond, find a place where the ice is thin, push up against it, break through, and go out on land where there is something fresh to cut and eat. After spring breakup time in March, the two young adults are expelled from the family group and forced to begin a long and dangerous journey in search of a place where they can find a suitable place to live and start a family.

In sharp contrast with the Snowshoe Hare, whose young are strictly on their own the day they are weaned and the next litter is on the way, young beavers have an unusually long training period. They stay with the family for two full winters, and when forced to leave, they are well able to care for themselves.

This year there are fewer voices in the spring choruses. The pond is becoming too large and too deep for the Cricket Frogs, Spring Peepers, Wood Frogs, and toads that prefer temporary pools as places to lay their eggs. As they did the year before, Leopard Frogs congregate to find mates and attach their egg masses to twigs and grasses, and again, Wild Turkeys wade into the water to hunt and eat them. A Great Blue Heron is also a regular visitor to that part of the pond.

168

Bullfrog, *Rana catesbiana*. This is the largest of the North American frogs. Mating season begins in early summer and the booming bellow of the male is a common sound around bodies of still water. Beaver ponds are ideal because they require bodies of water that do not dry up since it requires two full seasons for the tadpoles to mature.

Leopard Frogs can use temporary bodies of water for their tadpoles to develop. They are usually fully developed and able to leave the water by the tenth of July. Green Frogs, on the other hand, require permanent bodies of water. It takes a full year from egg laying until young frogs are fully developed, and with the Bullfrog, two full seasons are needed for the tadpoles to develop. Both species find the pond. In late May, the twanging sounds of the Green Frogs fill the air, and in late June the booming bellow of the Bullfrog is a common sound of early summer. Instead of being attached to underwater objects like those of the Wood Frog and Leopard Frog, egg masses of Green Frogs and Bullfrogs spread out across the surface, one layer thick, and in the case of the Bullfrog there may be twelve thousand eggs in each egg mass. The beaver pond proves to be an ideal habitat for Green Frogs and Bullfrogs for a number of years to come.

In the years before, several species of migrating waterfowl and wading birds saw the pond and passed it by. This spring again, Ruffed Grouse come off the hillsides to feed on the blossoms of alders and poplars. Woodcock again return to probe in the soft earth around the pond for earthworms and find places to nest. In the clearing around the pond this year they are joined by their relatives, the Common Snipe. The Woodcock is a bird of the open woods, while the Common Snipe is most at home in open, wet meadows. The snipes found ideal conditions in the new clearing around the pond.

A flock of Red-winged Blackbirds lands in the clearing, and some stay behind. Males claim territories and warn off rivals both by voice and by the display of their colorful capes. Females move in with selected mates, weave their nests, lay their eggs, and rear their broods of young.

In former years migrating Blue-winged Teal sometimes paid the pond brief visits. This year a pair remains behind. They did not arrive until after the other ducks had laid their eggs, and the process of incubation was well under way. The Blue-winged Teal is a typically North American species. Only slightly larger than the tiny Green-winged Teal, it is one of the smallest, swiftest fliers and greatest travellers of all wild ducks. Some winter deep in South America and are the last to arrive at their breeding grounds, often as late as May. The male is easily identified by a white facial crescent and a chalky blue patch on the forewing. The female is a little brown duck with a chalky blue patch on the forewing. This helps to distinguish it from the female Green-winged Teal.

The Blue-winged Teal is a ground nester, and the nest is always close to the water. It is a hollowed out depression, usually basket shaped and lined with dried grasses. One by one eggs are laid in it until they number about a dozen. The period of incubation is short, usually from twenty-one to twenty-three days. These little ducks are the last to arrive at the breeding grounds in the spring and the first to leave in the fall. By the time of the first frost the families are prepared to migrate south.

At about the time the teal is on her nest, the female beaver gives birth to four young. As he has done in previous years, the male moves out and lives apart from his family until later in the season. The beaver family now numbers ten.

The doe and the twin fawns of the previous year have been frequent visitors to the area of the pond. This year they are nearly as large as their mother, and lumps that rapidly increase in size appear on the head of one of them. He enters his second winter as a spike buck. At about the time that the young beavers are born, she gives birth to twin fawns again, and those born the year before are no longer welcome in the family group.

In former years migrating Blue-winged Teal sometimes paid the pond brief visits. This year a pair remains behind. They did not arrive until after the other ducks had laid their eggs, and the process of incubation was well under way. The Blue-winged Teal is a typically

North American species. Only slightly larger than the tiny Green-winged Teal, it is one of the smallest, swiftest fliers and greatest travelers of all wild ducks. Some winter deep in South America and are the last to arrive at their breeding grounds, often as late as May. The male is easily identified by a white facial crescent and a chalky blue patch on the forewing. The female is a little brown duck with a chalky blue patch on the forewing. This helps to distinguish it from the female Green-winged Teal.

Black Water Snakes begin to move into the pond to prey upon fish, frogs, and unwary birds. They, in turn, fall prey to Snapping Turtles, hawks, owls, and Great Blue Herons.

The muskrat is frequently referred to as "the little brother of the beaver." He is beaver-like in appearance and many of his habits, but he lacks the beaver's size and intelligence. He is tolerated by the beaver and has been known to go into the house with the beaver family. He takes full advantage of the works of the beaver, but instead of helping the beaver, his propensity for digging tunnels through beaver dams and letting the water out makes it necessary for the beaver to follow behind and repair the damage that he has done.

From the time that the pond was started, the muskrat population has steadily increased until the day that a mink and four half grown young move in and cause great consternation among the muskrats.

Male mink pictured in winter. The mink is larger than the weasel and smaller than the otter and is equally at home in the water, on land, or in the trees. It is the chief predator of the muskrat, eliminating the weak and unfit, and keeping the population within the carrying capacity of the range available.

They flee in terror in every direction. The chief victims are the young. The mink is the chief predator of the muskrats and keeps them from overpopulating their range. The muskrat is generally well able to protect itself from most enemies, but against the mink it has little chance of survival. The mink is an excellent swimmer and feeds on fish and frogs. It is equally at home on land or in the trees where it preys upon mice, squirrels, and birds. This mink and her young find the pond and its vicinity prime hunting territory and become frequent visitors.

Conditions in and around the pond are becoming stabilized. The dam is at its maximum height, and the pond at its maximum depth. Aquatic forms of plant life have been gradually increasing this year, and spatterdock or Yellow Pond Lily becomes firmly established. The changeover to an aquatic situation is complete.

There is unusual activity on the part of the beaver family: the pond bottom is cleaned, and the dam is made thicker and stronger. Water no longer flows; instead there is a well-developed spillway for the overflow. There are no longer stands of trees growing close to the pond, and it is necessary to travel farther inland to get them. Work is

Beaver pond in early March just after spring break-up showing some of the expanding edge conditions and one of the canals which radiate from a mature beaver pond.

172

begun on a number of canals, and every night they are made longer, wider, and deeper. In preparation for the fourth winter, the workers cut down, trim, and drag away another large stand of trees. The clearing around the pond is increasing in area at a rapid rate.

Maturity

The beaver family makes ample preparation for winter and survives it in excellent condition. After spring breakup the four young adults are expelled, and in May four kits are born.

In the ever-expanding clearing that results from the cutting down of trees by members of the beaver family, they create a condition which game managers refer to as "edge." In a dense stand of timber, food may be above the reach of many forms of wildlife, and in an open meadow where food may be plentiful, there may be no thickets in which to take refuge. In a typical edge condition, tall trees grade into saplings, saplings into brush, and brush into grassy meadow. Edge thus provides ideal conditions for many forms of birds and wildlife and a combination of places to find food and take shelter in close proximity.

This canal and a few other spots around an abandoned and empty beaver pond was the only water in this winter seen. The site had originally been a wooded area of trees approaching saw-log size before the beavers built their dam and flooded it.

173

In addition to the edge conditions at the margins of the expanding clearing, in the middle of it the beaver family maintains a pond that covers several acres of what was once forest floor. The pond approaches conditions of stability. In addition to the main pond, behind secondary dams downstream are backed-up bodies of water and a number of similar dams and bodies of water upstream. For over half a mile, the stream valley is terraced with dams and water impoundments that the beavers maintain. Radiating from the pond is a series of canals that are rapidly being made longer, wider, and deeper. The beavers have altered their environment to suit their own needs but in doing so, have created conditions where a host of other creatures find cover, food, and water close at hand and take full advantage of the situation.

As the pond grows in size, it becomes more heavily used by northbound migrating waterfowl in the spring and less so by those traveling south in the fall. As early as February, if there is open water, mergansers arrive, and from then until late April they are followed by northbound migrants that might nclude any species of duck found east of the Rockies. Some drop in briefly and then are gone. Others linger to feed and rest before winging their way north toward distant nesting grounds still held in the grip of winter.

Mother Mallard with young. The Mallard is a western species that has been moving east into territory that was formerly the breeding area of the Black Duck and is rapidly replacing it. Beaver ponds make ideal places to rear the young. This mother probably hatched twelve because she had six surviving when the photograph was taken.

Some of the ducks that come are residents which mate, make their nests, lay their eggs, hatch them, and rear their young. This year, a pair of Mallards stays behind and builds a nest and rear their young. This is a western species that is rapidly expanding its breeding range to the east and displacing the native Black Duck. The Pileated Woodpeckers abandon the nesting hole that they chiseled into the trunk of the dead elm. A pair of Wood Ducks finds it and occupies it. For the first time, a small flock of Canada Geese drops in and spends several days. They rest on the pond and graze on the grasses that grow in the clearing around it.

In addition to the ducks, coots, gallinules, and rails find the pond and take up residence. A pair of Pied-billed Grebes comes and builds a nest on the top of an abandoned muskrat house. As the clearing increases in size, so do the numbers of pairs of Red-winged Blackbirds that use it.

Young birds require large quantities of high-grade protein to grow and develop, and this exists in abundance in the clearing in the form of insect life. Ruffed Grouse and their young make brief forays from the shelter of the thickets to hunt for live things to eat. Female Wild Turkeys accompanied by groups of poults catch grasshoppers and forage for grubs, beetles, snails, and earthworms. After sundown their places are taken by mother skunks and their broods of young.

The skunk is a nocturnal member of the weasel family and is slow and clumsy in its movements. The skunk cannot overtake swift-moving prey, but it eats a wide variety of both animals and plants. The concentration of living things around a beaver pond makes them prime feeding areas for the skunk. All members of the weasel family have powerful musk glands. Those of the skunk are potent defensive weapons.

175

Where insect life is abundant, chipmunks and white-footed mice take full advantage of it. They also feed on a great variety of plant foods that include fruits, berries, and nuts. Also attracted to the clearing is a lemming-like creature, the Vole or Meadow Mouse. The Vole is a mouse-sized creature, gray in color, with a short tail and insatiate appetite. It is quite possibly the most prolific of all four-footed creatures. A female reaches sexual maturity at the age of one month, the male in forty-five days. Twenty-one days after she mates, the female gives birth to from four to eight young, and she mates again the day they are born. They are weaned when ten days old. A female may have up to thirteen litters a year which may total up to a thousand offspring.

A Vole is active both by day and by night. Each individual consumes its weight in food every twenty-four hours, and its chief importance to other creatures is its ability to rapidly convert vegetation into high-grade protein. Predators hunt it around the clock at every season of the year.

A pair of Northern Harriers or Marsh Hawks builds a grass-lined nest on the ground near one of the small upper ponds. In it the female lays four bluish white eggs. Both parents share the duty of incubation and the care of the young. The male is pale gray in color, the larger female streaked with brown. The birds alternately hunt the clearing, flying low in alternately gliding and flapping flight. In spite of size and color difference the white rump patch is the distinctive field mark by which members of the species may be identified. In addition to voles their diet consists of anything small enough to be caught and carried away. That includes frogs and insects.

This immature Screech Owl, gray phase, and all other members of the owl family find the clearings around beaver ponds prime hunting territories. With all members of the owl family, large and small, the meadow vole is the chief item of diet.

The hunting methods of the kestrels and Red-tailed Hawk are different from those of the harriers but no less effective. Instead of taking cruising flights across the clearing, they perch on lookout stations in conveniently located dead trees, and from their vantage points they use their superb eyesight to detect any sign of movement.

The abundance of potential prey attracts predators of every type. Bobcats, foxes, weasels, and mink include the pond and vicinity in their hunting territories and make periodic forays to seek prey. Raccoons are nightly visitors. They usually concentrate their activities along the watercourses and around the pond. Potential forms of prey find that the price of survival is ceaseless vigilance.

Water snakes specializing in preying upon fish and frogs are early arrivals at the pond. Later come Garter Snakes, Ribbon Snakes, DeKay's Snakes, Ring-neck Snakes, Brown Snakes, Red-bellied snakes, and Green snakes. With the development of the clearing and the buildup of the population of voles and mice, the Spotted Adder or Milk

Dead trees in and around beaver ponds make excellent lookout perches for hawks, like this young Redtail, hunting in the surrounding clearings.

Young raccoon feeling for crayfish in the stream. Because raccoons sometimes wash their food in water, many people believe that it is common practice. However, the raccoon usually eats his food wherever it is found or captured.

Young Cottontail Rabbit. The edge conditions created by the beaver ponds provide ideal habitat for these rabbits.

Snake appears. Its chief food is mice and rats, and it can follow them into their burrows. The Black Snake also appears to feed on mice, voles, moles, rabbits, eggs, birds, frogs, insects, and other snakes.

Over the years, the beavers have cleared a number of heavily used roadways that radiated out from the pond. These, in turn, fan out into numerous game trails that lead up the hillsides. One evening after sunset, the doe followed by twin fawns a couple of weeks old, comes off the hillside into the clearing. They are following the trail that they regularly use, but this time they are confronted by something new. Suddenly the doe stops. So do the fawns. She sniffs the air. There is a strange odor which carries a threat of danger. She snorts, stamps her feet, and comes closer. There is a sharp buzzing sound, and a four-foot Timber Rattlesnake issues a warning and draws itself into position ready to strike. The doe snorts and stamps her feet again, but the snake refuses to move. Suddenly, the doe leaps high into the air and lands on the snake with all four feet. She repeats the process several times, and her sharp hooves trample the rattler into a bloody pulp. The first Timber Rattlesnake to appear in the area in many years has made the mistake of being in the wrong place at the wrong time and paid for it with its life.

When the land was being cleared and settled, people considered rattlesnakes vermin and killed them on sight with the intent to exterminate them. Except in the most remote areas where small populations were able to survive, the plan was successful, and the rattlesnake was exterminated over most of its range. When the land was abandoned and nature reclaimed it, those small populations slowly increased their numbers and expanded their range until they reoccupied areas in which they had long been absent.

The Timber Rattlesnake is a deadly efficient predator. Instead of stalking its prey, it positions itself along a much traveled game trail and patiently waits until some unsuspecting warm-blooded creature approaches. When it is close enough, the snake strikes with deadly accuracy even in complete darkness, guided by the incredibly heat-sensitive organs housed in the pit below the eye and behind the nostril.

The top of the beaver dam provides a direct, convenient travel route that is frequently used by a variety of wildlife, large and small, which cross and recross the valley. As their feet and hooves compact the earth, it is sometimes necessary for the members of the beaver family to add new material. The newest users of this travel route are a Black Bear and her cubs of the current year. It is highly probable that these are the first bears to return to the valley since the land was cleared. As nature has reclaimed the land, small populations that survived in remote wild areas have slowly increased their numbers and expanded their range.

The bear family find the pond and vicinity a fascinating combination of playground and swimming pool and a delightful place to be on a hot summer afternoon. They spend many hours playing around and swimming in the pond, and their mother joins in with the play. The presence of the bears is sometimes resented by the beavers and to show their displeasure they swim round and round the

Large Black Bear photographed in a beaver meadow.

swimming bears. From time to time they slap the water with their tails. The sound startles the bears, but they soon become accustomed to the sound and ignore it.

Members of the bear family are not the only frequent users of the pond. In the early summer, swarms of pestiferous insects make life miserable for deer, who come down the hillsides to seek respite in the pond. At times, except for the tops of their heads and tips of their noses, they completely submerge themselves to drown out and rid themselves of their tormenters. Deer are also good swimmers and sometimes take refuge from enemies by jumping into lakes and swimming to safety.

They also take advantage of the pond in another way. Like the moose, they are fond of eating the Yellow Pond Lily. This year the young buck has considerably increased in size and weight and has grown a set of forked antlers approximately eight inches in length.

When the beavers first moved in, the sounds of the area were those typical of the woodlands: the drumming of the Ruffed Grouse, the woodpeckers' hammering out their Morse-code messages, the scolding of squirrels, and the calls of crows and jays. At sundown these sounds were replaced by the calls of Whippoorwills and the voices of

180

Screech Owls. By their works, the beavers have altered their environment to the point where woodland sounds have been gradually replaced by those typical of ponds and wetlands. Here, as spring advances into summer, the twanging sounds of the Green Frogs are gradually replaced by the basso chorus of Bullfrogs. Male Red-winged Blackbirds vociferously warn off rivals. The booming of the bittern mixes with the harsh squawks of other members of the heron family. There are the rattling calls of the Belted Kingfishers, the coaxing sounds of mother ducks calling their broods together. There are the voices of coots, gallinules, and rails and the strident calls of the little Pied-billed Grebes, all typical sounds of the wetlands.

In contrast with the clearing that attracts and supports an increased number and variety of living things, the ability of the pond to sustain and support aquatic forms of life has sharply diminished. In the early days when the pond was forming, Brook Trout were well fed, sleek, and full bodied. Now those that have survived are lean and big headed, both traits the unmistakable signs of malnutrition. The bottom of the pond is now carpeted with finely shredded wood which discourages the growth of bottom plants.

This autumn, the beavers again cut down and clear away another large stand of trees. They also lengthen, deepen, and widen their system of canals. In the winter that follows, despite the fact that many

Canal in early March that was started the previous season.

181

users of the pond have migrated south and others either slumber in snug dens or spend the cold months in the deep sleep of hibernation, the pond and its vicinity are the center of activity for many forms of bird and wildlife. Deer, hares, and an occasional Cottontail Rabbit make excursions into the clearing to browse on sprout growths from stumps and roots of trees that the beavers cut down. Wherever they or any others that pass that way travel, they leave behind complete records of their actions in the form of trails of footprints in the snow. Very often these document episodes of the grim drama of life and death, of predators in pursuit of prey: the dainty trail of fox footprints often leads past the spot where a startled grouse burst from its "form" in the snow; a set of tunnels left by weasels searching for mice and voles; heavy sets of footprints left behind where the feet of a bobcat churned up the snow as it attempted to run down a fleeing Snowshoe Hare; or again, the marks in the snow that bear evidence of a struggle when a Great Horned Owl struck down a hapless hare.

This winter is a low point in the lemming population of the Arctic tundra, and because of the scarcity of its natural prey, a Snowy Owl flies south until it arrives at the vicinity of the pond. There it finds the hunting good. This bird has a special advantage, for in addition to its ability to hunt at night, it also has excellent daytime vision.

This spring as usual, the young adult beavers are expelled from the pond. Greater numbers of waterfowl stop in to feed and rest, and many remain behind to seek out nesting places. However, as the pond approaches conditions of stability, its ability to produce a food supply for creatures living on or in the water decreases. In the middle of May, four more beaver kits are born and at about the same time, the doe gives birth to twin fawns.

In contrast to the decreasing ability of the pond to produce a basic food supply for the forms of life that use it, the clearing around it is producing food in increasing abundance. The beaver is noted for his ability to utilize a great variety of low-grade foods, but wherever and whenever those of high quality are available, he makes full use of them. This year there is an abundant crop of wild strawberries growing in the clearing, and members of the beaver family take full advantage of the opportunity. They make frequent trips onto the land to dine on them. The Black Bear and her cubs of the year before also discover that strawberries are tasty tidbits and spend many hours eagerly seeking them out. So also do deer, families of Ruffed Grouse, Wild Turkeys, and their poults find them welcome additions to their diets. Squirrels, chipmunks, raccoons, and mice take advantage of the opportunity to eat them as long as they are available as do catbirds, thrashers, robins, and thrushes.

The stumps, logs, and billets of wood that cluttered the clearing are rapidly being attacked by the forces of decay with the result that they create another major source of food for many creatures. Bacteria, fungi, and the larvae of wood-boring insects combine to break them down. Woodpeckers chip away the wood to get the grubs. Bears and other animals tear decaying logs apart to get them, and the rotted wood turns to humus that nurtures the growth of plants.

In late summer and early autumn there is an abundant growth of mushrooms in the clearing. These are eagerly sought by members of the beaver family and a great variety of other creatures. Toothmarks of squirrels on Deadly and Fly Amanita Mushrooms bear ample evidence that these species which are poisonous to man are eaten by some creatures with no ill effects.

When the beavers cut down trees, the clearing they create provides ideal conditions for woodchucks, and as it expands in size, the woodchucks that use it increase in number. There they find an abundance and variety of things to eat growing within easy reach. They dig a number of burrows at the edge of the clearing, and as the edge is

Adult hare shown in a summer meadow in an alert position. The price of survival is ceaseless vigilance. The hare was hearing a dog barking in the distance. It sniffs the air, pricks up its ears, and sits erect so that it can see above the tall grass.

183

moved back by the cutting down of trees by the beavers, some of these dens are out in the open. Woodchucks dig their burrows to make places to live, raise their families, and take refuge from enemies and inclement weather. However, these burrows also make it possible for many other species to survive. They are used for the same purposes by raccoons, skunks, cottontail rabbits, and on occasion by pheasants, and many other creatures take refuge in them.

Woodchucks have a number of enemies. Large hawks watch for young that have strayed too far from the safety of the den, and any that stay out after sundown risk attack from Great Horned Owls. Even though they are most active at night, bobcats are a constant threat.

On a higher point of land at the edge of the clearing there is a large woodchuck den. A pair of Red Foxes kills and eats the family of woodchucks that lived in it after which they take possession of the den and raise a family of four young.

The Red Fox finds the edge conditions around a beaver pond an ideal place to hunt for prey. It also feeds freely on the fruit and berries that grow there.

One evening after sundown there is an eerie sound heard for the first time in the area, a sound which, once heard, is never forgotten. The yapping howl of the coyote echoes across the valley. That sound proclaims the fact that the role of the Red Fox might suddenly change from that of predator to that of prey. It announces the arrival of a new, highly efficient, formidable predator possessed of a high degree of intelligence. Coyotes have moved east to occupy the ecological niche left by the elimination of the Timber Wolf. Today, the eastern coyote is larger and stronger than his western counterpart. He has adapted to life in the eastern woodlands as well as the open areas and is well established in the Adirondack mountain area of New York State.

Beavers, Wild Turkeys, and Snowshoe Hares have become reestablished in many areas because of successful live-trapping and transfer activities conducted by man. Whitetail Deer and Black Bears have returned because of protection given them by man. In

Whitetail Deer, eight point buck photographed in a beaver meadow in August with antlers fully developed but still in velvet. Exterminated in a large part of its range by 1840, it has now become reestablished as the most important big game animal in the eastern United States and Canada with man's help.

185

contrast, coyotes have extended their range in spite of every effort that has been made by man to exterminate them through bounties, traps, poisons, trained dogs, and long-range killing by high-powered rifles. Today in the east they are regarded as valuable fur-bearers.

The arrival of the coyote poses a new threat to members of the beaver family and to all other creatures living in and around their ponds. In late summer the bear puts the cubs up a tree, walks away, and leaves them. She has taught them well the lessons of survival and from now on, they are on their own. Later she finds a mate and during the winter, deep in a snug den in a well-concealed location, she gives birth to another pair of cubs.

When the leaves begin to turn color, southbound migrating waterfowl drop in and spend several days before resuming their journeys. At the edge of the clearing, a number of saplings have had the bark rubbed from them. These "buck rubs" were made by the buck that had been a fork-horn the year before. He used them to rub the velvet from his antlers and continued the process until they gleamed like polished leather. This year his rack of antlers is massive and by eastern measurement totals ten points. Now he weighs in excess of three hundred fifty pounds, evidence that weight, size of the rack of antlers, and the number of points depend more upon the quantity and the quality of the food available than age. Under ideal conditions, bucks can reach their prime at the age of three or four years. This buck has found conditions favorable in the vicinity of the beaver ponds.

Old Age And Abandonment

This fall, the members of the beaver family prepare for winter as they have in previous years with one difference. They have to travel farther to find the trees that they need. During the winter, spring, and early summer, life generally followed the same pattern. Suddenly in mid-summer, with the adults in the lead, the entire family headed upstream and continued beyond the headwaters, crossed over the top of the divide, and followed another watercourse downhill in search of a set of conditions favorable for them to relocate.

During the years that they lived in the valley, the members of the beaver family had in effect, as the country expression goes, "eaten themselves out of house and home." They had cut down and used up the trees that grew a safe and convenient distance from their ponds. This covered an area within a roughly two-hundred yard radius of the main pond.

Even before the beavers moved out, nature was taking steps to reclaim the area that they had cleared. Wind-blown seeds, some from sources miles distant, had landed. Some found conditions adequate for their needs, germinated, took root, and were established by the time

Recently abandoned beaver pond, looking downstream. The dam has been breached and the main feeder stream in the foreground is beginning to cut into the silt on the pond bottom.

Closer view showing the depth that the stream has already cut into the bottom of the abandoned pond.

that the beavers left. These included cottonwoods, Quaking Aspen, White Pine, Hemlock, Yellow birch, ashes, and maples. In addition, birds and animals left behind in their droppings pits of wild cherries, seeds of juniper berries, blackberries, blueberries, and many others. Some animals even brought in seeds from burrs lodged in their fur.

The first signs that the beavers had abandoned their ponds were rank growths of sprouts of willows, osiers, alders, or mixtures thereof growing along the tops of the dams. These came from unpeeled branches and other live materials that had been used in the building of the dam. In addition, without the grazing of the beaver family, there was a rapid growth of vegetation in the clearing. Seedlings of trees, shrubs, and bushes competed with weeds and grasses for sunlight and room to grow.

The main dam that the beavers built was a very solid structure, and they left it in an excellent state of repair. Consequently, during the rest of the year, there was little change in the water level of the pond.

All beaver ponds have one thing in common: each one is temporary. Its life span may be brief, or it may last for a number of years, but in every instance its demise begins when there are no beavers to maintain the dam that holds back the water to fill it. They may have been killed by man or other predators, the pond may have filled up with silt and thus be abandoned, or as happened here, after the beavers cut down and used all the trees within a convenient and safe distance from the pond, it became necessary for them to move to a new location.

Restoration

The dam that the beavers left behind was a very substantial structure, but during spring runoff time a break develops in it which drains the pond, and during the summer, the stream cuts a channel down through the layers of silt and shredded wood that had formed a thick carpet on the bottom of the pond. Seeds that had lain dormant in the mud and others that had been blown in or carried in by birds and animals take root to form a lush beaver meadow.

At the end of the summer there is a dense hedge growing along the top of the dam, and like the pond bottom, the mud that had been plastered against the upstream side proves to be an ideal seed bed. Seeds sprout and a dense growth of vegetation develops.

Except for water that remains in the deep part of the trench immediately above the dam where the beavers had dug up material to build it and in the deeper parts of the canals, the pond is empty. Secondary dams are also breached, and the water impoundments behind them drain. Forces of disintegration are at work in the stick work in the dam. The house caves in, and the site is marked by a pile of decaying sticks.

Migrating waterfowl traveling south this year find little water in the place where the pond was, but they do find a rank growth of smartweed whose seeds are ripe and ready to eat. Heavy growths of sprouts from stumps and tree roots add to those from seedlings that became established in the clearing and create an extensive area where hares and rabbits find both food and cover. In addition, this occurs during the year of the peak of the Snowshoe-Hare population cycle.

During the winter, the drained pond bottom becomes a clear snow-covered area surrounded by a low-growing thicket, which in turn is surrounded by a heavily wooded area. There, where tall trees shut out the light, food is often either scarce or out of reach. As a result,

Scene of an abandoned beaver pond. The Red Maple at the left that was living when the beavers moved in is now dead. The former dam now has a dense hedge growing along the top, shown meandering through the center of the picture.

189

the thicket becomes a favorite feeding and gathering place for wildlife. As evidence of their presence and abundance, after a clear, bright winter night, the snow in the clearing is covered with masses of footprints of Snowshoe Hares that bear evidence that they congregated here under the light of the full moon to play their versions of the games of tag and leap frog.

In March, these events take a serious turn when males wage fierce battles to possess the females. The teeth and especially the hind feet of the Snowshoe Hare, with their strong and sharp claws, can become most formidable weapons, and losers are sometimes badly injured. Spots of blood, tufts of fur, and sometimes pieces of skin on the snow often bear witness to the battles that have been waged there. There are also frequent records in the snow of times and places where hares and rabbits have fallen prey to a bobcat, fox, coyote, or a Great Horned Owl.

The next winter there are no records in the snow of the midnight gatherings of Snowshoe Hares in the place where they were the year before. There are two reasons. First, the hare population plummeted from the its peak the year before to the lowest point of the population cycle. In places where the snow was covered with tracks, this year they can seldom be seen. The second reason is that the clearing has disappeared. A rank growth of vegetation has covered the pond bottom.

The pioneering species of plants that sprang up in the clearing and on the pond bottom after the beavers left follows an orderly succession marked by a fierce competition for sunlight, growing space, nutrients, and moisture. First, there is a rank growth of grasses. They are overtopped with weeds. Among them, competing for survival are seedlings of trees. Little White Pines and Hemlocks grow sideways as well as upward to shade the ground under them and discourage competition. Red Cedars grow tall and straight, reaching for the sunlight. Young hardwoods grow tall and spread out limbs to keep their heads above competing species.

The young trees in their struggle to survive become surrounded by a dense bramble of blackberries, raspberries, and wild roses—a situation of both competition and protection. They compete for space, but they also bear thorns that discourage the activities of browsing animals. They also bear fruit which attracts many types of birds and animals, including bears, deer, raccoons, Wild Turkeys, and Ruffed Grouse. Also among the brambles are high bush blueberries, which bear luscious fruit. As a result, the area is crisscrossed with heavily used game trails. In the meantime, amid the bramble thicket, young White Pines, Red Cedars, and hardwoods struggle to survive and grow rapidly enough to reach the sunlight.

Abandond pond two years later. The picture was taken in late summer and shows the former dam and the dense hedge growing along the top.

The bramble thicket represents a stage in the plant succession. It, in turn, gradually becomes overtopped and yields to growths of Staghorn Sumac and hawthorn whose spines protect it from browsing animals. The haw apples are eaten by deer, grouse, and many other creatures, and the fruits of the sumac are a favorite food of many birds.

In time, the trees that manage to survive grow tall enough to overtop the sumac and hawthorn. Because of the shade that they produce, the sumac and hawthorn gradually die out as does all undergrowth of any kind. There follows a dense growth of saplings interspersed with an occasional White Pine or Red Cedar.

The roots of heavy growths of vegetation along the banks locks the soil in place, prevent the stream from widening or meandering, and confine it to the channel that it has cut through the layers of silt on the pond bottom. Between the well-defined banks, the stream runs clear and because of the shade, cooler. Prominent among the species that grow along the stream banks are thrifty young sycamores that spring up from water-borne seeds deposited by spring freshets.

A recently repaired beaver dam with brush growing out of the top of the older parts. These growths are sprouts from the living twigs and limbs used in the building of the original dam. Willow, Osier, and Alder are among the most common species represented.

Reoccupation

In the area that the beavers cleared, there is fierce competition to determine which trees will dominate. By the time that the trunk diameters of the dense growths of saplings attain or exceed three inches, conditions are ideal for a pioneering pair of beavers to move in. If so, they might repair the break in the old dam and restore it, or it is equally probable that they might start one in a new location. In any event, if left undisturbed, their pond will go through the same life stages as the former, or any other beaver pond. Its life span will repeat the stages of birth, infancy, adolescence, maturity, old age, and eventual abandonment. Over the centuries, the same sites have been periodically occupied, abandoned, and reoccupied.

The hypothetical set of conditions surrounding the activities of the beavers that moved into this valley, built their dams, maintained the ponds, raised their families, and eventually moved out do not take man into account. In most situations trappers decimate or exterminate them. Of necessity, the area where they live must be a location where they are completely free from any interference by man. Losses to predators

192

The beaver bank house at the center left of the picture and the canal at bottom right are on a natural lake in the vicinity of Tupper Lake, New York.

have not been considered, and no attempt has been made to follow the fates and activities of the young adults that were expelled from the family group. Each one faces an uncertain future as it wanders in the presence of enemies, in search of a place to make its home. Nevertheless, all the events described here could well have taken place within the space of a normal active beaver lifetime.

The beaver is a remarkable animal. No creature except man surpasses him in his ability to change his environment to suit his special needs. He builds dams, maintains ponds, clears roadways, digs canals, and conducts extensive logging and lumbering operations. These things he does in order to survive, but the dams he builds spread out flood waters, slow them down, and reduce their capacity to do damage downstream. The ponds store water against times of scarcity and act as settling basins for silt carried downstream during periods of high water. The clearings around the ponds let in light and create edge conditions. Wherever beavers build their ponds, a vast variety of living things are attracted to them as iron filings are drawn to a magnet.

193

References

1. Allred, Morrell. *Beaver Behavior: Architect of Fame and Bane.* Naturegraph. Happy Camp, California. 1986.

2. Babcock, H.L. *The Beaver as a Factor in the Development of New England.* Bulletin of the Boston Society for Natural History 37. Boston. 1925.

3. Bailey, Vernon. *Beaver Habits and Experiments in Beaver Culture.* United States Department of Agriculture Technical Bulletin No. 21. United States Government Printing Office. Washington, D.C. 1927.

4. Bradt, G.W. *Michigan Beaver Management.* Michigan Department of Conservation. 1947.

5. DeKay, James T. *Natural History of New York, Zoology Section.* Thurlow Weed. 1842.

6. Grasse, James E. and Euveren F. Putnam. *Beaver Management and Ecology.* Federal Aid in Wildlife Restoration Project Wyoming 31D and 30R. Second edition. Wyoming Game and Fish Commission Bulletin No. 6. Cheyenne, Wyoming. 1950.

7. Grescham, Bert. The Beaver. "The Hudson's Bay House." Winnipeg, Canada. c. 1944.

8. Grey Owl. *Pilgrims of the Wild.* Charles Scribner's Sons. New York. 1935.

9. Grzimek, Bernhard. *Grzimek's Animal Life Encyclopedia.* Vol. 11. Mammals II. Van Nostrand Reinhold Co. New York. 1975.

10. Hanney, Peter W. *Rodents: Their Lives and Habits.* Taplinger Publishing Company. New York. 1975.

11. Hodgdon, Kenneth W. and John H. Hunt. *Beaver Management in Maine.* Reprint of second edition (1955). Department of Inland Fisheries and Game. Augusta, Maine. 1958.

195

12. Jordan, David Starr. *Manual of the Vertebrate Animals of Northeastern United States.* The World Book Company. Yonkers-on-Hudson, New York. 1929.

13. Mills, Enos Abijah. *In Beaver World.* Houghton Mifflin Co. New York. 1913.

14. Morgan, Lewis Henry. *The American Beaver and His Works.* J.D. Lippincott and Company. Philadelphia. 1868. [Reprinted in 1986 by Dover Publications, Inc. (with a new introduction by Robert J. Naiman). New York].

15. Richards, Dorothy. *Beaversprite, My Years Building an Animal Sanctuary.* With Hope Sawyer Buyukmihci. Heart of the Lakes Publishing. Interlaken, New York. 1983.

16. Skinner, Constance Lindsay. *Beaver, Kings and Cabins.* The Macmillan Company. New York. 1933.

17. Smith, Kenneth C. *Beaver in Louisiana.* Louisian Wild Life and Fisheries Commission. n.d.

About the Author

Earl was most fortunate in his early years. When he was five years old, his family moved out of Rochester, New York, to a small crossroads community eight miles to the west, known as Parma Corners. There he spent a large part of his time on, in, and around his father's mill pond and along the small creek that fed the pond. At an early age, he became keenly interested in fishing and other outdoor activities and developed a lifelong fascination for things related to the outdoors. At the same time he developed a serious interest in history, especially American history. His combined interests in the outdoors and in history played a major role in the organization of the book, *Beavers: Water, Wildlife, and History*. Earl had another advantage: parents who shared his interests and encouraged him in every way.

197

After graduation from high school he attended the University of Rochester where he majored in biology and received a Bachelor of Arts degree. At a later date he received a Master of Arts degree from New York University.

After graduation from college he taught biology for a number of years in high schools in New York State. He also spent several summers as a nature counselor in Boy Scout camps.

It was when he was on the staff of the Rochester Museum of Arts and Sciences that he became involved in the planning and the collecting of specimens for a beaver diorama. It was here that he first came in contact with the beaver and his works. From that time on, his interest in this incredible creature has never diminished.

During the later years of World War II, he was the motion picture photographer for the New York State Department of Conservation. During the years that followed the war he traveled widely as a wildlife photographer, film lecturer, and film producer. Films that he has produced are in libraries across the country. His original films are now in the archives of the International Museum of Photography at the George Eastman House in Rochester.

During the years that he was traveling as a film lecturer, he made several thousand personal appearances for clubs, schools, colleges, in theaters, and on television. For seventeen years he traveled with his films as a speaker for the National Audubon Society across the United States, Canada, and in Nassau and Bermuda. In those appearances, he stressed the importance of the beaver in the conservation of water, soil, and wildlife.